MULTI-AGENCY RESPONSE TO VIOLENCE AGAINST WOMEN

State of the State: MAHARASHTRA

MULTI-AGENCY RESPONSE TO VIOLENCE AGAINST WOMEN

Feminist Social Work within the Police System

TRUPTI JHAVERI PANCHAL
VINITA AJGAONKAR

Vitasta
LET KNOWLEDGE SPREAD

Special Cell for Women and Children
Resource Centre for Interventions on Violence Against Women

Published by
Renu Kaul Verma
Vitasta Publishing Pvt Ltd
2/15, Ansari Road, Daryaganj
New Delhi - 110 002
info@vitastapublishing.com

ISBN 978-93-86473-50-9

First Edition 2019
MRP ₹995

Editor: Papri Sri Raman
Cover: Somesh Kumar Mishra
Layout: Ram Kumar
Cover painting by Aneri Jhaveri
Printed at Chaman Enterprises

Dedicated to the women of Maharashtra

— the brave, the violated, the survivors, those who have mustered courage to speak out, social workers, psychologists, police officials, university faculty and families—each and everyone who has helped create Special Cells, supported and sustained them and contributed to reducing violence against women.

Contents

Acknowledgements

The authors and the Resource Centre for Interventions on Violence Against Women, Tata Institute of Social Sciences, thank the following people, without whom the writing and publication of this work would have been impossible:

Women survivors of violence who came to the Special Cells, shared their experiences, and are the driving force behind the Cell and its mission.

The Department of Women and Child Development, especially Mr CB Turkar (Deputy Secretary); The Maharashtra Police, especially Ms Sridevi Goel and Mr Prabhat Ranjan (both DIG – PAW); and the Tata Institute of Social Sciences for support and guidance.

Social workers and coordinators of the Special Cells over these years, who have been the backbone of the programme and were instrumental in collecting and monitoring the data which went into this publication: Amrapali Dalvi, Anagha Sarpotdar, Anita Pagare, Anjali Shelke, Anjali Bole, Anupama Gokhale, Archana Kale, Archana Puyed, Archana Rasal, Arpita Das, Asawari Jadhav, Deepa Gaikwad, Deepali Kedare, Deepak Patil, Deepali Mankar, Deepali Tompe, Divya Taneja, Gayatri Patil, Kamini Sonavane, Karuna Mahantare, Laxmi Jadhav, Laxmikant Kamlajkar, Maya Waghmare, Meenakshi Chavan, Meenakshi Yamgar, Megha Gaikwad, Monika Sonawane, Nikhat Sheikh,

Neeta Kute, Neha Bhandare, Nutan Abhang, Papita Waghmare, Pekham Basu, Poonam Suryavanshi, Pradeep Rathor, Pradnya, Pratibha Gajbhiye, Pratibha Jagtap, Pratibha Kachevar, Pravin Mahire, Priyadarshani Kolpate, Radha Gaware, Rahul Wasnik, Rajani Lokhande, Rajashree Ambare, Rani Date, Ranjana Gaikwad, Renuka Kad, Rashmi, Rekha Suroshe, Sangeeta Aahire, Seema Dhavale, Sanjeevani Arwel, Sanjay Telrandhe, Sheetal Kambale, Shraddha Mohite, Shraddha Jadhav, Shrikant Niwal, Sitaram Shinde, Sujata Jadhav, Surekha Rankhambe, Suchita, Suresh Suryavanshi, Suvarna Joshi, Suvarna Patil, Tikendra Khelkar, Urmila Jaykar, Vandana Nanavare, Vrushali Athale, Vaishali Ranade, Vijayashree Gaikwad, Yogesh Patil, Jyoti Pipal, Indira Pawara, and Jyoti Sapkale.

Special Thanks to Project Counsel Professor Anjali Dave and members of the RCI-VAW Team, who helped with editorial support, feedback, collecting testimonies and providing support and encouragement: Melita Vaz, Radhika Chakraborty, Yashoda Pradhan, Taranga Sriraman, Manisha Kande, Sandali Thakur, Shama Shaikh and Sweta Marodkar.

Finally, many thanks to the publishers whose encouragement motivated us to finalise this work and place it in the public domain.

Foreword

Padma Shri Indira Jaising

Trupti Panchal has authored a book we have been waiting for, an evaluation of the function of the Special Cells in Maharashtra, the birth place of similar such Cells across the country. It needs pointing out that the first of the cells was started in 1984, almost simultaneously with the introduction of Section 498A IPC. It was natural, therefore, for the cells to be located in the police stations, though they were not a part of the Police Station.

The women's movement in India, for some time before 1984, had been doing case work on domestic violence and had by then accumulated a good deal of experience on the feminist ethics of case work. It was a time when dowry death cases were not investigated and were recorded as 'accidental deaths'. It was the consistent advocacy of the mothers of the women who died that led to the passing of Section 498A IPC.

Hence, when the first Special Cell was established in 1984, there was a body of feminist counselling that the cell workers could depend on. Coming as they did from TISS as trained social workers, the Cells were successful as outreach centres for women in distress who were approaching the police stations.

The Special Cell for Women and Children (also referred to as the Special Cell or the Cell) began as a strategic collaboration between the Police System and the Tata Institute of Social Sciences, Mumbai (TISS) to provide a multi-agency coordinated response to violence against women and children.

Social workers sat at the police station and offered support to women survivors of violence as emotional support and counselling, legal advice, referral and linkages, support in filing a police complaint, information on how the criminal justice system works, or advocating on their behalf to families and support systems.

We are now accustomed to seeing women's cells in police stations but in the beginning, the most unique feature of the approach was its location within the police system. The location was chosen after studying the patterns of help needed. Women appeared to go to the police stations as their first port of call. Moreover, it was and is the mandate of the police to protect citizens from violence. Police services are meant to be constantly accessible to all citizens, due to the spread of police stations and their 24-hour mandate.

However, as we all know, police stations are not the only port of call of women and many approach their families, or their neighbours or friends or an NGO or in serious cases, a hospital. Different models have emerged in these other locations.

While the police addressed the immediate problem, the social workers in these Special Cells took care of the long-term problems of the survivor, building her self-confidence and self-worth.

The Special Cells work on following values:

- **Self-determination:** where a woman is encouraged to make informed choices.

- **Individualisation:** where the rights of a woman and her choices irrespective of her relationships with other persons are appreciated and recognised
- Acceptance of women with non-judgmental attitude
- **Participation** of the woman in the problem-solving process
- **Confidentiality and Privacy**

These continue to be the guiding principles of all socio-legal cells, wherever located.

Over the years useful data has been collected on gender of the people approaching the Special Cells – their Educational background, the nature of violence, mental, physical, financial, substance abuse-triggered violence, sexual, desertion. These special cells also work as the resource pool for the scientific information based on data collected by them and analysed by the researchers to understand the behavioural patterns of violence and thereby come up with mechanisms to tackle the same.

In 2005, with the passing of the PWDVA, all forms of violence was recognised by the law and a new channel of access to civil justice was opened for women facing violence. Under the PWDVA, the woman was given a choice to choose between criminal or civil legal action against the perpetrators of violence against her. For the first time, not only the violence by husband or his relatives was recognised but also the violence faced by women at their maternal homes was given its due weightage. The 2005 Act provided a total of 5 different kinds of interim reliefs to women. It did not just focus on punishing the accused but providing relief to the destitute woman. The Act provided for interim residence order, stop violence order, compensation order, custody order and maintenance order. The Special Cells took this development on board and provided counselling to women, which was tailored as per their needs.

These Special Cells have a different way of dealing with civil and criminal cases. In some cases, the women are also referred to outside NGOs for counselling, after they have decided that they do not want to peruse the matter legally. In case the woman decides to file under the PWDVA Act, the Special Cells do the hand-holding till the very end. In case where the woman decide to file a criminal case, the fact that Special Cells are set up in proximity of the police stations, helps the social workers track the record of criminal cases these survivor women file and see them to their end.

The book also elaborately discusses the expansion of these Special Cells from 10 in Maharashtra to every district of the State. A pilot project, which was started with just 1 cell initially and grew to 10, has today become a huge success not just in the State of Maharashtra but all over the nation, as it has been adopted by other States too. From 10 cells, in the year 2005 the Department of Women and Child Development began its expansion to 40 special cells. In 2013 the Maharashtra State Government sanctioned the setting up of these Special Cells from 40 to 144. Currently these cells have also been functioning in States of Uttar Pradesh, Rajasthan, Delhi, Gujarat.

Dillasa

While the growth of special cells is indeed impressive and the author has been pioneering the projects not only in Maharashtra but also in many other parts of the country, other models of multi-agency response have also emerged in the country. Dillasa, located in a hospital in Mumbai, has been hailed as a 'best practice for woman approaching a public hospital', where women go for medico-legal help. The hospital location has enabled the administration to take ownership of the centre and proceed to train all medial and para-medical staff on the need to treat violence against women as a public health issue.

Nirbhaya Fund

Much later and after the Nirbhaya rape and murder, a Nirbhaya Fund has been set up by the Central government to fund the prevention of violence against women. The Ministry of Finance, GoI provided an initial corpus of Rs 1000 cr (as per the announcement in Budget 2013-14) for women's safety pertaining to the strategic areas of prevention, protection and rehabilitation. For subsequent financial years of 2014-15 and 2015-16, an amount of Rs 1000 cr (each financial year) have been provided under the Nirbhaya Fund.

One Stop Crisis Centres (OSCCs)

Setting up of the One Stop Crisis Centres for providing shelter, police desk, legal, medical and counselling services to victims of violence under one roof, integrated with a 24-hour Helpline was a recommendation of the 12th Plan Working Group on Women's Agency and Empowerment under the guidance and supervision of Justice (Retd) Usha Mehra. One-stop crisis centres are being funded all over the country and in part funded by the Centeral government, one in each district. There is no doubt that one in each district cannot serve the purpose, but it is a small beginning and we await the evaluations of these newly-established centres. The Government of India has left it to the States to decide the location of the Centres and there is a lively debate on where they can be best located.

Bharosa

On a recent visit to the Bharosa centre, we saw yet another model in operation in Telangana. Bharosa is located in rented premises by the Commissionerate of Police in Hyderabad, it is neither located in a police station nor a hospital, nor a shelter home. It is unique in being run by a society registered under the Societies Registration Act. It is located on the doorstep of the POCSO court. It employs a central administrator who is well qualified in social sciences and full-time clinical psychologists. It houses emergency medical services. The centre has the full commitment of the police and is 'driven' by the police. Every woman approaching the Police Station is sent to the Bharosa center, irrespective of the kind of legal procedure the woman wants to follow. In cases where the woman does not intend to file an FIR, she is sent to the Bharosa centre for counselling and other immediate reliefs in terms of medical or social assistance. In serious cases of rapes and violence, the woman is sent to the Bharosa center after the FIR is filed. As Bharosa has an emergency medical room which has been given the status of a government medical unit, she is given her medical treatment and evidence is collected, which, through IO, is then sent to the Forensic lab. Funding comes from the police budget and some portion from the Safe Cities Funds of the Women and Child Development Department. The links with the police station are clear and women and children are assisted in filing FIRs, and the cases are monitored from the commencement to conclusion.

There have been other models of One Stop Crisis Centres which are not in the Police Stations or the Hospitals such as:

Rape Crisis Centre in Delhi

The Delhi Commission for Women is implementing the Rape Crisis Cell Programme for Women since 2005. The standardised protocols between the RCC and the Delhi Police were established in 2009.The Crisis Intervention Centers also function under the Rape Crisis Cell of the Commission. The Delhi Commission for Women invites applications from leading NGOs with a legal background to run the Rape Crisis Cell and Crisis Intervention Centres. Currently, the Association for Development (AFD) is entrusted with the responsibility of running the RCC. AFD is a pioneering organisation with long experience of over 20 years in the field of women's rights and more particularly, rehabilitation of sexual assault victims. The Rape Crisis Centre is situated in the office of the Delhi Commission of Women and supervises Crisis Intervention Centres (CIC), which are run by 10 NGOs and are present in every district in Delhi, where counsellors are employed.

Court-based One Stop Centre (OSC)

In order to facilitate the best humane, psychological, medical treatment to the victims of crime during investigation, i.e. crime and thereafter, it is important to have support services at the level of the court. It is a known fact that there is a complete absence of support to navigate the court procedures, understand the court procedures and its implications, and provide support and hand-holding throughout the court procedures. This necessitates the establishment of a court-based OSCC. Such an OSCC has been established by the Delhi State Legal Services Authority (DLSA) since 2016. The Centre is functional since 31.03.2016. One judicial assistant and one orderly are posted in the Centre. Psychological/emotional counsellors sit for a few hours on weekends or come in when the Centre has prior notice of a victim. The Centre is primarily used for recording of statements of minors and victims of sexual offences by Magistrates u/s 164, CrPC.

While location is one issue, there are more significant issues to be dealt with, such as the following of Standard Operating Procedures for staff of the One Stop Crisis Centres, which have been published by the Ministry of Women and Child Development of the Government of India and the observance of medical protocols also published by the Ministry of Health, Government of India, sensitive to the needs of women and children.

I have learnt a lot from this book and also from the author who is a pioneer in the field of social justice. She and her colleagues have shaped the debate on multi-agency responses to domestic violence in this country, from which many of us have grown. It is a meaningful contribution to our knowledge, enabling us to assist women in distress

Padma Shri Indira Jaising,
former Additional Solicitor General of India
Delhi, February 2019

Special Message

Sridevi Goel, DGP (Retd)

I first got to know of the Special Cell for Women and Children through the Maharashtra State Taskforce on Violence Against Women when I was working as Deputy Commissioner of Police (Port), Mumbai city in the early 1980s. These were the early years of the Special Cell. Later, in my capacity as Deputy Inspector General (Prevention of Atrocities against Women), I was associated with the Special Cell again. At this time, the social climate had begun to focus on the issue of violence against women and heated debates about it rocked our parliament. The government realised the need to increase the outreach of the Special Cell programme so that more women facing violence in private or in public life could avail of the service.

The Special Cell was not only involved in working directly with violated women. It also realised the need to make the Police more sensitive regarding this issue and training them on how to work on the matter. The social workers took up the task of training the Police and other key stakeholders. I was closely involved with these efforts. Even though I was not DIG (PAW) any longer, when the Memorandum of Understanding was signed between Maharashtra Government, TISS and UNIFEM, it warmed my heart to know that I had been a part of such a historic process. Eventually, this led to the Special Cells being a regular part of the police system in Maharashtra.

It is my firm conviction that having trained social workers within police stations helps to strenghen the response of the Police to crimes against women. I am happy to see the work of those momentous years of expansion described in this book and to see how it has served the women who need it the most. I wish all the members of the Special Cells another ten years of even better work and greater achievements.

Sridevi Goel
Director General, Home Guards (Retd)
Maharashtra Police
Mumbai, February 2019

Preface

Violence Against Women first came to be viewed as a serious social problem in the early 1970s, in part because of the emergence of the Women's Movement in India and the world over. It is one of the most widespread human rights abuses, affecting on an average one in three women and girls worldwide. It is endemic to all communities and in its various forms cuts across caste, class, race, age, religious and national boundaries.

According to the United Nations Declaration, violence against women includes 'any act of gender-based violence that results in, or is likely to result in, physical, sexual or psychological harm or suffering to women, including threats of such acts, coercion or arbitrary deprivations of liberty, whether occurring in public or private life (United Nations, 1993)'.

The most common type of violence against women worldwide is 'domestic violence' or the physical, emotional and/or sexual abuse of women by their intimate partners or ex-partners (Lori L Heise et al, 1999). There are other forms of violence, such as dowry harassment and violation of women's right to inherit property which are linked to traditional or customary practices and are limited to specific regions and communities, especially in the Asian context.

It is only now, through the sustained activism by women's organisations, that violence against women, including domestic violence, is starting to receive substantial attention nationally and internationally. As domestic violence becomes increasingly recognised by state and non-state actors and discussed today, important questions are being raised concerning its magnitude in different settings, and its causes, consequences and related risk factors and in response to this, strategies to eliminate violence against women are being developed.

In order for survivors/victims to get the best support possible, their rights, needs and safety must be placed at the forefront of all interventions. This means offering protection and support when women at risk need it most, treating them with respect and sensitivity, and empowering them to make informed decisions that best reflect their interests. There is a need to have multi-or inter-agency coordinated measures and to implement them by way of effective cooperation among all relevant actors playing a role in preventing and combating violence against women and domestic violence.

Likewise, there is increasing recognition of the need for better data on the effectiveness of different interventions. In India, access to justice is one of the foremost issues for women, as it often translates into consistent improvement in services available to them. Due to the limitations of service-based data, accurate figures on the prevalence of domestic violence/ violence against women must be obtained through putting together information from women who approach services and are asked directly about their experiences of violence. This data is used to obtain important insights into some of the consequences of violence and risk factors associated with violence and in the long term, to monitor trends and to explore the impact of different interventions. On the other hand, more in-depth qualitative case studies provide a means for obtaining greater insights into the settings and contexts in which violence occurs, the dynamics of abuse, and to better understand how women, children and communities are affected by this violence. Likewise, documenting, studying and theorising, working with and engaging violent men in the process to end VAW, can provide important insights into the causes of violence, help in developing strategies to respond to and work with men and assess the impact of different forms of intervention.

This book will focus on one such strategy, the Special Cell for Women in Police Stations, developed to respond to VAW in the context of Maharashtra.

Since its beginning as one Special Cell at the Police Commissioner's Office, over the years the project expanded to more police stations, first within the city, and then across the State as a grants-in-aid programme of the Government of Maharashtra.The Special Cell programme has now evolved as a national movement. **Figure 1** represents the expansion of the Special Cells over 30 years, tracing its journey from its inception in1984 to 2016.

Growth of the Special Cells Programme in Maharashtra

Figure 1: Key Historical Milestones

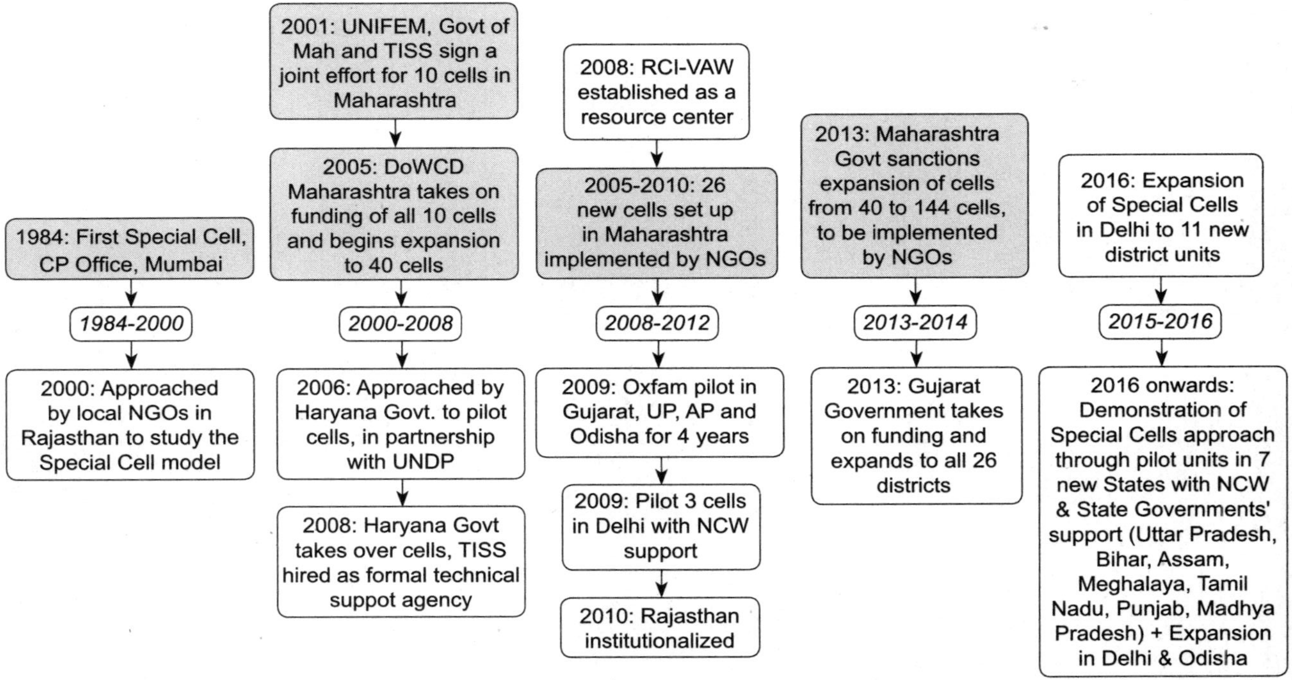

The Special Cells model gained momentum throughout the 2000s, with the Maharashtra government taking over and successively expanding cells from 10 to 144, and pilots implemented in five other States between 2006-2009

Introduction to the Special Cell for Women

The Special Cell for Women and Children (also referred to as the Special Cell or the Cell, or Special Cells) began as a strategic collaboration between the Police System and the Tata Institute of Social Sciences, Mumbai (TISS), to provide a multi-agency coordinated response to violence against women and children.

The first Special Cell was set up on 2nd July 1984 at the Office of the Commissioner of Police, Mumbai (then Bombay), with the purpose of working for social justice and equality in the context of gender relations, particularly on the issue of violence against women and children. Since its inception, the Special Cells have expanded both within Mumbai, and to the districts of Maharashtra State. Beginning with referrals from the police, and gradually building and growing to expand services and establish its practice; today there are 144 Special Cells for Women and Children sanctioned in Maharashtra, along with Special Cells for Women in 14 States across the country. All the Special Cells for Women and Children are located within the police system. The *Special Cells work with a clear understanding that violence against women is a crime,* against both the survivor and society, and it is a crime against the state. It is, therefore, the responsibility of the state to prevent and counter this crime.

The premise of the Special Cell at its inception was deceptively simple: social workers would sit in a police station, and offer support to women survivors of violence who approached the police system, with whatever services they may need – emotional support and counselling, legal advice, referral and linkages, support in filing a police complaint, information on how the criminal justice system works, or advocating on their behalf with families and support systems. The dearth of such services – at the interface of the state and the justice system with an explicitly pro-woman approach – made this intervention deeply relevant and unique.

Since then, the practice of the Special Cell has strengthened and grown, to consolidate and build upon the foundations of feminist social work praxis, and advocate for the expansion of supportive State-based services for women survivors of violence. The focus of the Special Cells in its current form remains in keeping with its roots – asking a woman survivor 'what she wants' and through feminist social casework, ensuring her right to make her own choices and live a violence-free life.

This book seeks to document the journey of the Special Cells for Women & Children in Maharashtra State, following the first major period of its expansion from 2002 onwards; and, as mentioned above, focus specifically on the growth and consolidation of feminist social work practice at the Special Cells over these years. It will explore monitoring data, case studies, testimonials from clients and stakeholders, and narratives from social workers, to build a holistic picture of the work of the Cell, its impact on violence against women, and challenges faced by survivors and stakeholders.

Special Cells' Perspective on Violence Against Women

THE SPECIAL CELLS' perspective on the issue of violence against women and children and its ideology governs and directs the methodology with which its services and programmes are designed and implemented. The perspective that the Special Cell is based on is that the various forms of violence against women widely prevalent in society are a manifestation of patriarchy, which is a characteristic of Indian society. Patriarchal society recognises a woman in terms of her relationships with men, perceiving her as a daughter, sister, wife, and mother, and *does not recognise her as an individual in her own right.*

Patriarchy structurally excludes women from the decision-making process in various arenas of life, both within and outside the family. Gender inequalities promote violence against women within their families as well as in society. In patriarchal societies, the nature and extent of violence against women is a widely prevalent phenomenon. In such societies, violence against women occurs irrespective of their socio-economic class and religious background. *The Special Cells' experiences of intervening on the issue of violence against women over several years indicates that the widespread occurrence of violence on women is a result of societal rather than personal factors.* In those contexts where gender inequalities are extreme, violence against women takes on a gruesome nature, which includes female infanticide, wife battering, harassment for dowry and dowry deaths, sexual harassment at the work place, rape, child sexual abuse and other such crimes. The family, the state and the community play an important role in the perpetuation of violence against women by either actively perpetuating it, or by passively ignoring it.

Interface with the Police

One of the most unique features of the approach is its location within the police system. Location within the police system is a deliberate and strategic intervention, which serves a number of important functions. The police is the first formal state agency that most women experiencing domestic violence are likely to approach, as it is the mandate of the police to protect citizens from violence. Police services are meant to be constantly accessible to all citizens, due to the spread of police stations and their 24-hour mandate. Therefore, women in crisis situations who have sought help from non-state agencies but not found support that ends the violence itself, turn to the police to seek help for stopping the violence in their lives.

However, the services available with the police are often not adequate to answer a violated woman's needs. The training that police personnel undergo is not oriented to help them understand the requirements of the survivors of violence, nor does it provide them the specific skills required to help these women come out of abusive situations. More often than not, most police personnel have a patriarchal mindset, a product of their training and social conditioning, that prompts them to encourage women to compromise and adjust to the violent situation in the interest of protecting the unity and sanctity of the family. In a patriarchal system, the family is sacrosanct. For the understaffed and overworked police force, therefore, violence against women (VAW) becomes a low priority issue.

Thus in 1984, there was a felt need to create a space within the criminal justice system where women experiencing violence could have access to social services provided by trained social workers. Women require support in navigating the criminal justice system and advocating for their right to a violence-free life. The state has a responsibility to address violence against women, and the Special Cells' goal is to support the woman survivor, as well as urge the state to take ownership and responsibility for the delivery of women's rights. The result of this need was the establishment of Special Cells directly within police stations, with the belief that harnessing the strengths of the police system, along with the skills of trained social workers at the Special Cells, will enable a coordinated, multi-agency response to the issue of violence against women.

The Mission Statement for the Special Cells[1] emphasises that the collaboration of the Special Cell and the police system enables the needs of the violated woman to be addressed holistically in the following ways:

- The police system addresses the legal aspects, and the Special Cell works with the psycho-socio-legal aspects of violence.

---

[1] Compiled by Mahtani R and Panchal T. Mission Statement and the Monitoring Indicators for Special Cell for Women and Children - A Programme for Curbing Violence Against Women Within the State Police System, TISS (2004).

- The police system addresses the problem in the here-and-now, while the Special Cell engages in problem-solving by taking into account the context and history of the violated woman.
- The police system accepts the woman's context of violence as a reality and uses state power to contain the violence and to protect the woman. The work of the Special Cells is focused on bringing about a change in the violated woman's position and situation, with the aim of empowering her to protect herself and her rights.

The Special Cell believes that the state bears the responsibility for preventing violence against women. The location of the Special Cells within the police system underlines this belief. The social workers in the Special Cells can constructively use the legitimised and sanctioned power and authority of the police to push for an end to violence against women at the individual and societal level. At the same time, the Special Cell can seek civil remedies for potentially socio-legal cases, such as restoration of rights to property and access to the marital home. The Special Cell links the police system with women's organisations and other social service groups, thereby enhancing a coordinated response to the violated woman's needs.

Working from within the police system and in police spaces has helped the Special Cells' social workers to understand the police's structure, day-to-day functioning, environment, procedures, rules and limitations. This understanding helps them to effectively harness the scope of existing laws, rules and regulations, and to create spaces that are safe and valuable for women survivors. Constant interactions between the social workers and the police help in identifying areas that need to be strengthened or changed in order to facilitate a more sensitive response by the police to VAW. In 2003, at an international conference on Women and Police in Brazil, the Maharashtra police acknowledged the value of such system-based responses by describing the Special Cell as the 'Police's Felt Need', – validating the rationale for locating the Special Cell in the police system (Dave 2015).

Though the Special Cell is located within the police, it is not a part of the police force force. The Special Cell workers function with a clear understanding that the Cell is not an alternative or substitute to the police and police services; and functions autonomously from within, but in partnership with, the police.

The methods, values and principles of the Cell are distinctly different from the values of the police. The relationship of the Special Cell with the police is thus built on a shared interest and a commitment to responding to violence against women. Institutional grounding – of the Special Cells for Women & Children in Maharashtra – within the Tata Institute of Social Sciences, has been crucial to maintaining this position of autonomy from, as well as location within, the police; and this has also enabled the Special Cell to contribute to, and draw from, the latest academic discourse. The Special Cell thus finds itself at the intersections of the system, academia, as well as the women's movements globally.

Structure, Values and Approach

Applying a survivor-centric and human rights-based approach in supporting women is not only necessary in order to fulfill international and constitutional state obligations, but is first and foremost necessary to make sure that victims seeking help feel truly supported by the Special Cell interventions. When receiving protection and support, women should not in any way feel disrespected, patronised, judged or pressured. Hence, the values of social work and feminist practice, along with harnessing state authority for the violated women are all very crucial.

Every Special Cell unit located in a police station, or office of the Superintendent of Police (SP), consists of two trained social workers with post-graduate degrees in Social Work, who provide services and support to women clients. The social workers may be women, or man-woman teams. The monitoring, supervision and handholding of the Cells is the responsibility of the Special Cell coordinators, each of whom is responsible for administering ten Cells.

The police provides other infrastructure for the Special Cells, such as furniture, telephone, and vehicles, apart from providing space within the police location for the Cell. This ensures the police too have an active commitment and stake in the programme. A Steering Committee chaired by the Additional Chief Secretary, Home has been set up to monitor, facilitate and develop the programme. Its members are drawn from the Directorate of Women and Child Development (DWCD), police, NGOs and TISS.

The Special Cells' work draws from the values, principles and interventions of social work practice, which foreground a commitment to the most vulnerable and marginalised in society. The social work principles at the Special Cell are grounded in practice and decades of experience, as well as being rooted in core feminist social work values. These values can be identified as follows:

- **Self-determination**: where a woman is encouraged to make informed choices and decisions about her own life

- **Individualisation**: where a woman is respected and recognised in her own right as a person, and not on the basis of her relationships with other persons, for example as someone's daughter or wife
- Acceptance of the woman with a **non-judgmental attitude**, irrespective of her choices and behaviours
- **Participation** of the woman in the problem-solving process
- **Confidentiality and Privacy**

The Special Cell's work is based on a pro-woman perspective, which recognises that the woman survivor of violence is not responsible for the violence inflicted on her, and that within patriarchal society, the misuse of power by men makes her vulnerable to violence. Further, Special Cell workers act on the premise that violence against women is not a personal matter to be resolved by the family alone; but is a social issue that needs to be addressed in the public domain (Mahtani & Panchal 2004).

The Special Cell works at the individual as well as at the systemic level. Its work includes the following:

- Working with individual women survivors of violence to help them combat the violence in their lives.
- Working with various community groups to bring visibility to the issue of VAW.
- Working with government and non-government agencies to build recognition of the needs and rights of survivors of violence, as well as to promote effective interventions by them in the interest of the violated women.
- Networking with the police, criminal justice system and NGOs to build support systems for the women survivors of violence.

- Undertaking research and documentation to enhance understanding of the issue of violence against women and to promote the effectiveness of the programme.

One more essential aspect of the Special Cells' ideology pertains to the fact that its work draws from the values, principles, methods, and interventions of professional Social Work practice. Human beings are central to social work methods and interventions, which are based on the belief that all human beings can change, including both the oppressed and the oppressor. Thus, Social Work practice is built on the premise that a planned problem-solving process can bring about social change, as human beings are resourceful and have potential for transforming their own lives.

Social Work practice is committed to marginalised and vulnerable stakeholder groups, and the Special Cells' commitment to violated women is in accordance with this, as violated women are marginalised. Thus, the role of trained social workers in carrying out the work of the Special Cells is another essential component of its ideology of work, which is focused on process-oriented social change.

The objectives of the Special Cells are based on its ideology of work.The Special Cells' work is directed towards:

- Rebuilding the violated women's self-esteem, self-worth and dignity,
- Offering immediate services in cases of family violence and atrocities against women in the forms of:
- Police assistance in registering complaints,
- Placement in institutions or referral to family service agencies,
- Counselling,
- Referrals to other services including medical, psychiatric, educational and vocational,

- Legal Aid,
- Liaising between police and organisations for women and children,
- Creating awareness about the humiliations and atrocities committed, particularly against women and children, amongst women themselves, professional groups, and the general public, and
- Documenting the work of the Special Cells and developing training materials for social work students and police personnel.

An Overview of Special Cells Services/Programmes

The Special Cells' services and programmes are based on its ideology of work and its objectives. An overview of the services and programmes of the Special Cells is presented diagrammatically:

Figure 2 Services and Programmes of the Special Cells for Women*

Women survivors & Children	Police System (Police Personnel, Police Patils, MTNKs & MDS)	Other Organs	Community Groups
Negotiating for non-violence with stakeholders	Building alliances with the police and other systems in the interests of violated women & children	Creating an environment of acceptance of the human rights of women, especially violated women	Creating an environment of acceptance of the human rights of women

Promoting the rights of women with systems and stakeholders	Building awareness in the police & other systems on the violated woman's problems & perspective	Building awareness in organisations on the problems & perspective of violated women	Building awareness in community groups on the violated woman's problems & perspective
Building the violated woman's self-confidence & self-esteem	Training police & other systems on issues pertaining to violence against women		Training community groups on issues pertaining to violence against women
Empowering violated women	Harnessing police authority to help violated women		
Building support systems for the violated woman			
Enabling the violated woman access services, resources & assets due to her			

* Rajshree P Mahtani, Executive Summary Report of 'Strategy Planning for the Special Cells for Women and Children: an Action Research Project (2002–2005)' 2006.

The Special Cells' process of interventions is primarily directed at the individual level of the violated woman, with a focus on immediate crisis intervention, as usually a violated woman seeks help at the time of a crisis.

Subsequent to immediate crisis intervention, if the woman desires, the Special Cells' interventions focus on her longer-term development. Women are helped to think critically, be assertive and develop a positive self-image. They are helped to relocate themselves in a new set of social circumstances. While working at the individual level with the violated woman, the Special Cells also intervene with her families, neighbourhood, community, kinship groups, the police and other components of the Criminal Justice System, the health system etc. so as to develop understanding of the situation of the violated woman and garner support for her.

Partnering with the Police

The Special Cells' **intervention at the level of the police system** in the interests of the violated woman is directed towards both problem-solving on specific cases of violated women and working towards attitudinal and systemic change at the level of the police system. The police system is an organ of the state that is essentially responsible for the management and containment of violence, along with the criminal justice system.

However, police personnel are not socially neutral, as they are also socialised according to patriarchal gender norms, as are other members of society. Further, the training given to police personnel is not aimed at making them gender-sensitive. The police function as gatekeepers within the criminal justice system by selectively deciding upon whether or not a reported incident requires police attention. *In the experiences of the Special Cells, the police do not offer unconditional protection to all women against all forms of male violence.*

On the one hand the police may choose not to intervene in a 'domestic' situation, as they often perceive violence to be a natural or typical expression of the male-female relationship. On the other hand, some police personnel may identify with the man accused of violence by a woman, and thus, they intervene on his behalf instead of the violated woman's. *By refusing to entertain women's complaints, police can, and do effectively legitimise male violence on women.*

By intervening at the level of the police system, the Special Cells aim to sensitise police personnel on the status of women, family violence, and other aspects of the issue of violence against women in society. The Special Cells also acquaint police personnel on the nature of social investigations required for crimes against women and the available supportive services for women.

The Special Cells simultaneously carry out interventions at the level of the police system in two ways. One of these is to continuously discuss specific cases of violence against women the Special Cells are working on with police personnel at the local level. The other is to intervene at the macro level of the police system as a whole by organising training programmes, orientation visits to police stations etc. All these interventions at the level of the police system are aimed at preparing the police to offer unconditional protection to women against all forms of violence.

Social Work Education

Two other aspects of the Special Cells' services and programmes pertain to their **interventions with other organisations,** and **with the community** in the interest of violated women. These are aimed at creating an environment of acceptance of the human rights of women, building awareness on the violated woman's problems and perspective and providing training on the issue of violence against women.

Research and Documentation

In addition to direct work with violated women, and interventions at the level of the police system, organisations and communities, the Special Cells have also had a consistent **programmatic component of presentations, documentations, publications and intervention research** (**Annexure** 5), aimed at contributing to knowledge development on the issue of violence against women. This area of the Special Cells' work has also focused on contributing to social work education by integrating practice experiences into the teaching-learning process with regard to the issue of violence against women, and develop frameworks for gender analysis.

Early Days: Inception to Pilot Expansion

Since from the time of its inception till the present, the very identity of the entity 'Special Cells for Women and Children' has undergone a significant, periodic, structural change, in keeping with evolving societal needs of the times. From the time of establishing the first Special Cell in 1984 till 2001, the 'Special Cell for Women and Children' functioned as a field action project of the Tata Institute of Social Sciences (TISS) in collaboration with the Mumbai Police.

Between 1984 and 1994, the Special Cell had expanded from one to three in Mumbai (one each in the Office of the Commisioner of Police, Dadar Police Station, and Kandivali Police Station). In 2001, a tripartite Memorandum of Understanding (MoU, Annexture 4) was signed by the

Government of Maharashtra, UNIFEM and the Tata Institute of Social Sciences, wherein the Special Cells assumed the identity of a joint programme between the three partners, with a stated agenda of expansion to the other districts in Maharashtra State. This MoU was applicable for the period 2002 to 2005, and it pertained to the setting-up and functioning of a total of 10 Special Cells, including the three Special Cells that were already functioning in the city of Mumbai.

As a result of this MoU, it was expected that at the end of this phase of expansion, the Special Cells would become a part of the Maharashtra State, through the Maharashtra Police, after a joint review. A significant aspect of this expansion of the Special Cells was that the 7 new Special Cells to be established reaching women in the rural areas. Thus, under this MoU, the Special Cells expanded to seven districts of Maharashtra State, namely, Navi Mumbai, Pune, Yavatmal, Aurangabad, Nashik, Wardha and Nanded. Thus, during 2002 to 2005, the Special Cells for Women and Children functioned as a joint project of the Government of Maharashtra, the Tata Institute of Social Sciences and the United Nations Development Fund for Women (UNIFEM).

Within the Government of Maharashtra, the Department of Home and the Department of Women and Child Development were involved in the administration of the Special Cells project. A Monitoring Committee under the chairpersonship of Additional Chief Secretary (Home) was appointed to guide and mentor the project during this three-year period. By the end of 2005, on completion of the MoU, the Special Cells for Women and Children were scheduled to be taken over by the Department of Women and Child Development, Government of Maharashtra as a 'regular administrative measure'.

Institutitonalisation of the Special Cells within the Police System

The Special Cells field action project focused on developing a strategy for the Special Cells, so as to address issues related to the expansion of the Special Cells within the police system. In order to think and and plan for the components pertaining to a variety of issues and concerns related to the ongoing expansion and anticipated institutionalisation of the Special Cells within the Maharashtra police system, a core group was formed to undertake a Strategy Planning Exercise to take certain critical decisions for the service.

The Purpose, Process, and Outcomes of Strategy Planning

A core group was formed called Strategic Management Group (SMG) for the purpose of Strategy Planning pertaining to effectively addressing the issues related to the expansion and institutionalisation of the Special Cells within the police system, and to ensure long-term effective provision of services for violated women in the State of Maharshtra.

Also, it facilitated the clear articulation of the Monitoring Indicators which made the work of Special Cells measurable/ tangible. These indicators provided the police with a tool to understand the work of a Special Cell and monitor it.

In order to ensure that the experiences of the Special Cell interventionists as well as field experts are taken into account, the SMG comprised TISS Faculty in Charge of Special Cells, a Coordinator and two senior social workers led by an external consultant and facilitator. This process was crucial at this juncture in the Special Cell's journey, as the future structural relationship between the Special Cells, the government and the police system had to be worked out for the smooth functioning of the Special Cells.

The SMG worked on several aspects of the programme so as to recognise that there continues to be a strong need for trained social workers to look into the socio-psychological aspects of the needs of violated women within the police system.

The aim of the Strategic Management Exercise (SME) was to develop a mission statement for the Special Cells that would ensure a common ideology across all the Special Cells, which would guide their operational functioning, in keeping with the required quality of work across all the Special Cells, based on the collective experience of the Special Cells.

The SME also aimed to review implementation of strategy by setting-up a monitoring system, including the development and specification of monitoring indicators. These monitoring indicators have been used as a guiding document to train social workers as well as to introduce the work of the Special Cell in a detailed manner to various stakeholders.

Along with documenting and consolidating the work of the Special Cells, the SME also aimed to address the issue of institutionalising the Special Cells within the police system, so that they become an integral and permanent part of the system. The SME also brainstormed over the concerns related to the expansion of the Special Cells, especially those pertaining to managing a larger number of staff members and develop a Strategy Plan for the Special Cells Special Cell, for the duration of the MoU.

During the Strategy Planning Process, the SMG considered the five possible options with regard to the future structural relationship between the Special Cells and the government and the police system:

- institutionalising the Special Cells as a State-sponsored autonomous body, similar to the Mahila Samakhya model,

- institutionalising the Special Cells as a part of a department of the government,
- institutionalising the Special Cells as a government scheme to be implemented by non-governmental organisations,
- registering the Special Cells as an independent women's organisation, or
- continuing the Special Cells as a field action project of the Tata Institute of Social Sciences in collaboration with the Maharashtra police.

The implications in terms of the advantages and disadvantages of each of these options were considered by the SMG, and it suggested that in the present context (India post-2000), the most appropriate structure for institutionalising the Special Cells is to do it as a State-sponsored autonomous body, similar to the Mahila Samakhya* model. But eventually the State chose the third option of NGO-implemented Special Cells, a franchise model.

In 2005, through Government Resolution number DWCD GR No. 2005/Pra.Kra.19/Ka.2 dtd. 05.12.2005, the Maharshtra cabinet approved the institutionalisation of Special Cells for Women & Children as a Government programme to be established/expanded in a phased manner in all districts of Maharashtra.

Existing 10 Cells were taken over by the State administration as part of the said institutionalised programme, and ten more were established as per GR dtd. 17.10.2006. Currently, there are 144 Special Cells functional across Maharashtra.

---

* The Mahila Samakhya programme was launched in 1988 to pursue the objectives of the National Policy on Education, 1986. It recognised that education can be an effective tool for women's empowerment.

The Significance and Process of the Evaluation Study

In order to ensure that the service delivered at the Special Cell is of good quality and to find out if the primary beneficiaries of the services, the violated women, find it of value, before the expansion of the Special Cells took place, it was decided that an evaluation study would be conducted by an external expert.

The State had committed to take over the Special Cells as an administrative measure after a review of the 10 Special Cells under the tripartite MoU. The monitoring indicators developed during the SME were used to frame the research design for the evaluation study. The research led to impact-based expansion towards a 'regular administrative measure' by the government for curbing Violence Against Women. The evaluation was the clinching evidence which brought the government to take the decision to expand the service. An external expert was appointed to undertake the evaluation study in 2003, just one year after the new seven Special Cells were set up in the districts. Some of the highlights of the study were the following findings:[2]

> **Who is She?**
>
> The profile of the woman coming to the Special Cell is about 25 years old and she is married, with a child (30% had child marriages).
>
> She has had some exposure to education, contributes to family income in some way but **has almost no assets** (over 90% with no savings or house).
>
> She **has already approached her family**, network or community before she comes to the Cell.
>
> Most women have either been **referred to the Cell by ex-clients** and word of mouth (36%) **or police** (25%).
>
> 20% of the women are non-literate and 30% come from rural areas.

[2] Statistics are from the evaluation of 10 Special Cells in Maharashtra for the year 2003.

What Kind of Violence Has She Faced?

Women coming to Special Cells have faced severe abuse from their husbands and families. The 2003 data revealed:

92% of women visiting Special Cells had faced physical violence; 32% got medical help for their injuries.

As a result of violence, 78% of women coming to the Cell were not living with their husbands.

Domestic violence was the overwhelming reason for which women came to the Cell, **80% were beaten by their husbands** while 36% were beaten by their families.

9% of the women had attempted suicide, and **the husbands of 25% had attempted to murder them.**

What are Her Expectations?

On their first visit to the Special Cell, a majority of women are looking for the Cell worker to **intervene with their husbands** (75%) **and expect a non-violent reconciliation** (62%).

Over 90% expected some kind of relationship intervention while 9% came for information.

Despite severe violence, 20% wanted divorce and only 5% wanted to prosecute, while many wanted help in getting their legal rights such as maintenance income or their own property and belongings.

Over 30% of women wanted police intervention to stop the violence.

How Does the Special Cell Help Her?

Special Cells provide women with a much needed support system, **listening to the woman, engaging her in the problem-solving process** and directly interacting with the perpetrators of violence.

Women felt '*emotionally understood and light*' (75%) and '***strengthened***' (50%) **to deal with future incidents.**

In most cases, **Cell workers met with the husbands** (74%) and also met in-laws (28%).

Women felt empowered; they were prepared to contact the Cell (56%) or the police (42%), while others referred women to the Cell (54%).

A year later, **violence had reduced for 20% of the women who came to the Cell.**

How did the Special Cell impact the violated woman's feelings?

More than 90% women felt that the **Cell worker heard them sincerely** and had understood their problem.

They felt that they were given **respect and focussed time and attention,** and felt like **returning to the Cell** (76.9%).

According to 77.2% of the women, the **approach of the Cell workers to problem-solving** was among the biggest reasons why the woman wanted to return to the Cell for problem-solving.

73.3% women said that they gained **significant amount of information** on what to do and what not to do in case of violence and got to know the various options available to them from which they could make informed choices. This shows that availability of reliable information too is very very scarce for the Indian woman.

Were women satisfied with the services at the Special Cells?

57.4% women were **satisfied to a great extent**. They felt that they got appropriate help (in getting belongings, streedhan, divorce), moral support, got strength to be self-reliant. Mental harassment by husband and in-laws reduced considerably. Marked positive difference in the behaviour of the husband was visible.

31.4% women **were somewhat satisfied.** They felt that the Cell worker understood the problem and provided the requisite support but the problem was only partially solved.

9.6% women were **not at all satisfied.** Here, none of the expectations of the women were met.

Considering the complexity of the problems for which women approach the Cell, infrastructural limitations, limitations of judiciary, police, time and personnel, the positive response from women is heartening.

Did Women Want to Come Back to the Special Cells?

93.4% women felt that they **would like to revisit** the Cell for help in case of further need in future.

An overwhelming percentage (92.7%) of women felt that they would **recommend the services of the Cell to other women** and many of them have already done so.

Carrying forward the same trend, **92.7%** clients conveyed that it was **essential to have the Special Cell within the police** system, because they felt that women alone could understand women's problems. They believed that this was required to fight injustice needed for women who have no support system available. Just as the police invoke fear, paradoxically, the police also invoke a sense of strength and protection in the general citizenry.

Features of the Special Cells

- Giving visibility to the issue of violence against women;
- Legitimising the violated woman's concerns and needs within a pro-woman perspective;
- Simultaneity of working at the individual and systemic level, within the context of trained social work practice; Developing a strategic alliance with the police system for a more coordinated, coherent and in-depth response to the issue of violence against women, with the aim of integrating social services for the violated woman within the police system;
- Engaging the violated woman in problem-solving.

Open House

Besides the evaluation study, the Special Cell has also developed a method of getting to meet the ex-clients through an event called the Open House. The Open House has been created for women who have sought help from the Special Cell in the past years to meet the social workers with whom they had developed a relationship, as well as meeting other clients of the Special Cell to share their experiences, joys and sorrows.

The Special Cell workers organise games, posters and documentaries at the venue, designed to give the women new insights, create awareness and promote bonding with other survivors of violence. The Open House is also a space for women to give feedback about the interventions they had received at the Cell, and share whether these brought about the desired change in their situations, or had an impact on their lives. It helps maintain continuity in the relationship between the Special Cell and the woman, while at the same time strengthens the response of the Cell to the woman. Several women also chose to come with their husbands and families. This indicates that the Special Cell, through its intervention, is able to engage with men and not create a hostile environment for them.

Advocacy with State to Bring Special Cells to Talukas

The period from 2003 to 2012 witnessed exciting growth for this woman-centric service. Recognising the worth of the programme, in 2009 the Mumbai High Court had ordered the expansion of this service to talukas. In Criminal Appeal no. 359 Sou. Ratnabai Jaising Patil vs. State of Maharashtra (Annexure 1), the High Court invited Tata Institute of Social Sciences as an expert to give suggestions on how to strengthen work to prevent violence against women.

At present, there is State government sanction for 144 Special Cells, including those in districts and taluks. The programme is currently implemented jointly by the Department of Home and the Department of Women and Child Development (DWCD), Government of Maharashtra – a shift from the original collaboration directly between TISS and the police force. Under the present programme, local non-government organisations (NGO) implement the Cells in different districts, through a 'franchise model'. With the expansion of the Special Cells, the role of TISS has evolved into one of coordination and monitoring. TISS also directly oversees the implementation of 14 Special Cells.

Impact of the Special Cell

The Special Cell has proved to be an effective demonstration of working within the criminal justice system and of a multi-agency response to violence against women.

- Over a period of 10 years, Special Cells have grown from 3 in number in the city of Mumbai to 123 across the State of Maharashtra. The number of women who have sought support in TISS-implemented Special Cells have increased from 919 cases in 2002 (with 3 Special Cells) to 3,987 cases in 2017 (with 14 Special Cells). See Annexure 2 & 3 for more details on number of cases received and addresses of the Special Cells implemented by TISS.
- There was recognition of the effectiveness of the strategy of working with the system, especially with the police, by the United Nations Special Rapporteur on Violence Against Women in its India report in 2002. The Special Cell made a presentation to the United Nations Special Rapporteur on Violence Against Women in April 2013, making recommendations on legal reforms in rape laws, opposing the proposed changes in the 498A Bill, emphasising the need to strengthen social services within the police system and the office of the Deputy Inspector-General-Prevention of Atrocities on Women (DIG-PAW) and pointing out the limitations of the all-women police station strategy being adopted in various States.
- The Special Cell has played a key role in formulating the Protection of Women from Domestic Violence

Act (PWDVA) 2005, in giving training inputs and in advocating for increased budgetary allocation for implementation of the Act. The Special Cell is also recognised as a Service Provider under the Act in the State.

- The Special Cell has fought for and won judgments protecting privacy of women clients of the Cell and confidentiality of the intervention process (Rajesh Dharap vs. Deputy Commissioner of Police. Mumbai/ Registrar and Deputy Registrar, TISS).
- The Special Cell, along with other NGOs with experience of dealing with cases of VAW, is invited for participation in *lok adalats*, a pre-litigation forum recognised by the courts.
- Through an intervention petition filed in court in 2012 (The State of Maharashtra vs. Vijaysingh Chandrasen Shinde & Anr.), the Special Cell sought and achieved validation of the legality of the programme's existence, location and work. The intervention petition also accelerated the expansion of the Cell and set into motion the process of increased resource allocation to the programme.
- The experience of the Special Cells of working with violated women has been invaluable in curriculum development at its home, that is, at TISS itself.

Resource Center for Interventions on Violence Against Women

After having anchored the work of Special Cell for Women & Children in Maharashtra State, building on and disseminating the cumulative experience of intervening in cases of VAW through research, advocacy and wider work in collaboration with the State for over two decades, a need was felt to consolidate the entire body of work and learning. This idea then took shape in

2007-08, in the form of the **Resource Centre for Interventions on Violence Against Women (RCI-VAW)**, based in TISS.

The RCI-VAW was envisioned to resource the existing Special Cells for Women & Children – i.e. to assess and address internal training & research needs in particular – as also to inform practitioners and policy-makers about the larger discourse and praxis in responding to VAW in India. From the start, this was supposed to be done by pursuing a steady engagement with the issue of VAW, by initiating, innovating, supporting and nurturing effective interventions on VAW with different stakeholders through training and modelling, as also through steady research to enable deeper understanding of the issue and intervention/s to stop VAW.[3]

In the context of continued expansion and replication of Special Cells, however, the role of TISS and the RCI-VAW in particular, has simultaneously expanded into demonstrating direct and effective intervention on VAW in collaboration with the police in different regional contexts, through innovative strategies and then facilitation of the process of institutionalisation within the governmental system, as well as doing the same with non-governmental stakeholders (agencies/organisations/groups). For more details on the multiple models through which RCI-VAW has expanded the work of Special Cells in different States, see Annexure 3.

As the process of expansion of the Special Cells in Maharashtra and the demonstration efforts in other States gathered momentum, a greater need for training, capacity-building and handholding of the new workers began to be felt. A key element of the advocacy and capacity-building was to constantly reiterate and promote the core elements of the social work intervention at the Special Cell. The importance of

[3] First draft concept note of the RCI-VAW (2007).

action-research as the cornerstone of advocacy in the specific issues related to violence against women, and for the purpose of updating and innovating the intervention strategies of the Special Cell, was also realised.

Initially conceived of as a *centre for research* on violence against women, the erstwhile Centre for Research on Violence Against Women, set up in 2000 by a grant from the Ford Foundation, sought to create a library of resources on violence against women, and also produce research on violence against women. The focus of this centre soon developed into generating and collating resources specific to *interventions* and that which will be useful for interventionists in their practice.

Several key studies were produced by this Centre in the initial period (about the nature of violence faced by lesbian women, a study of family counselling centres and short-stay homes, a study on the profiles and perceptions of Special Cell, customary remarriage practices of *nata* in Rajasthan; amongst others) which reflected this focus.

In 2008, Resource Centre for Interventions on Violence Against Women (henceforth RCI-VAW) came into being formally, to more clearly reflect the focus on intervention in order to generate resources which would strenghthen VAW services, conduct trainings to develop expertise in interventions to stop violence against women and develop strategies for advocacy for the expansion of the Special Cells programme. In the context of continued expansion and replication of Special Cells, the role RCI-VAW has grown into is that of demonstrating and implementing pilot Special Cell models in collaboration with the police in different regional contexts through innovative strategies. Besides, it facilitates the process of institutionalisation of the Special Cells and advocating for State governments to take ownership of the programme.

Insights from the Decades of Growth and Expansion

THE SPECIAL CELLS' journey has been a long and rewarding one – starting from one Special Cell in the Police omissioner's office in Mumbai, to the programme's current presence in fourteen States across India. We hope to continue growing in the coming decade and deliver quality socio-legal services to women survivors of violence across the country. This book is an account of the processes and impacts of the Special Cells' expansion in Maharashtra, and explores the quantitative impacts of the work from monitoring data, as well as testimonies from survivors and stakeholders.

It picks up after the evaluation study of 2003 and presents an account of ten years of work following the first successful push for growth. As we are poised to begin working in even more States, it seems fitting to take this opportunity to reflect on the past decades of work in Maharashtra, the birthplace of this now-national movement, and take our cues from this long journey to plot a roadmap for the future. Here I share a few highlights of the reflections on my own journey with the Special Cells, and my vision for its growth and development.

The Seeds of Growth: Understanding the System

The Special Cells for Women and Children began as a field action project of the Tata Institute of Social Sciences, to provide social services to women survivors of violence from within the police system. The first Special Cell began with just two social workers, in 1984 in the office of the Commissioner of Police in Mumbai. From the very beginning, we emphasised the right to self-determination of the woman, and the importance of hearing the woman's voice.

Our initial years were spent in understanding the system, syncing and adapting our process with that of the system to address its specifications, establishing our patterns of work and evolving effective strategies of working with women. It takes time for people from outside the system to demonstrate successfully to the Home Department the efficacy of an intervention or idea. Still, it is creditable that after merely four years, the Commissioner of Police (Mumbai, then Bombay) authorised the first expansion to the Dadar Police Station in 1988 because he found this work useful.

Expansion has always been on our agenda, but things do not always work out as planned. For instance, the Thane Special Cell began in 1988 but shut down in 1989. The experience of a Cell shutting down taught us what was required to set up a Special Cell and then to sustain it. When the Kandivali Special Cell started in 1994, I was the social worker placed there. We did a lot of ground work at that time, and that experience served me well when we expanded into the other districts of Maharashtra.

It has always been our firm conviction that the State should ultimately adopt this as a government programme. So, from year one, we started presenting proposals to the State government, but the government always raised issues of funding and of having no budget. *There was never sufficient political will to bring violence against women on to the front burner.* The police system is also a difficult system to convince. On the ground, we had already done a lot of convincing, because they could see the direct usefulness of the work, but we needed to undertake more visibility exercises to reach out to people in power who could make decisions. Despite these hurdles, we were able to establish cells in Dadar and Kandivali.

Critical Partnerships and Milestones

Soon, in the 2000s, we were able to turn this situation around. One major breakthrough for us was obtaining support from the UNFPA in 2000; an outcome of advocacy work by Prof Anjali Dave, then Project Director. Through this partnership, in 2001 we were able to expand further, and started two Special Cells in the Police stations in Thane District – in Ulhanagar, and then in Dombivali in 2002. UNFPA had provided funding, because at that time, the discourse centered on VAW as a public health issue. We were attempting to explore if we could be located within the police and coordinate with the health system. But these objectives could not translate into reality the way we expected. We tried to work with the municipal hospital and also undertook training programmes with the local health system and with the local corporators, but despite these efforts we were not able to make significant inroads within the health system. However, these efforts provided us with key learnings regarding the processes of expansion, which served us well in later years when we were able to grow further in Mumbai.

Around this time, a task force was constituted to deal with the issue of violence against women in the State, under the aegis of the Additional Chief Secretary, Home. It had members from the police force and from the Home Department. Tata Institute of Social Sciences was invited to be a member of the task force from 1999 onwards. In one of these meetings, we were able to present the model of the Special Cell, which had worked well in Mumbai.

The years 2002 to 2005 were very critical for us, as during this time the police were leading the Special Cells from the front. Our earliest supporter had been the then-Police Commissioner of Mumbai Julio Ribeiro; and even during this phase of expansion the police offered support by providing funding. Sridevi Goel, then Deputy Inspector General-Prevention of Atrocities against Women (DIG-PAW), Maharashtra Police was one of our strongest allies. Prabhat Ranjan, another source of strength, became the DIG later.

Expansion accelerated in 2002. A Memorandum of Understanding was executed between United Nations Development Fund for Women (UNIFEM), the Home Department, the Department of Women and Child Development (DWCD) and TISS (Annexture 4). A condition in the MoU was that the government would review the progress after three years, with a view to making it a regular government-funded programme. The proposed review after three years took the form of an evaluation study. The evaluation study was conducted by an external expert and was placed in the public domain in 2003.

This study was a key milestone, as it showed that women survivors who had used the services of the Special Cells were satisfied with the services received to a very high degree, and validated our years of work and struggle for space within the system. It was through documented proof of effectiveness that we were able to convince the State government of both, the feasibility of the project as well as the overwhelming need for it at the community level.

The government taking ownership of the Special Cells after this, marked another milestone in our journey. This was what we had wanted all along – that the government should recognise the need for such services across the board and adopt such services.

Government officials recognised that rather than the Home Department, this work fitted within the mandate of the DWCD, which had the funds for it. The DWCD had prior experience of working with NGOs and proposed a franchise model for the Special Cells – bringing in several women's groups and NGOs across the State to take ownership of Cells in different districts and localities. Thus, along with the change in funding from the Home Department to the DWCD in 2005, this was another turning point for the Special Cells.

Till this point, police ownership had always been very strong, but from this point it became less so. Looking back, I would like to acknowledge that it was not only the destination that was important, our journey to reach that point was also deeply enriching.

Our expansion took place in two phases. The three existing Cells in Mumbai, at Commissioner of Police' Office Mumbai (Crawford Market), Dadar police station and Kandivali police station, were taken over by the government. We were requested to start seven more Cells: Special Cells at Navi Mumbai, Nanded, Aurangabad and Pune were established in the first phase, that is, by mid-2002, and at Yavatmal, Nasik, and Wardha in the second phase, in 2003.

The districts where Cells would be located were identified by the task force. The then Deputy Inspector General of Police, in-charge of Prevention of Atrocities Against Women (DIG-PAW)

Sridevi Goel, set parameters such as crime rate, accessibility, and rural-urban distribution. Yavatmal was selected as it is from the tribal belt. Nanded was identified as a key Grade-B city. Pune Rural Police Station was prioritised over Pune Urban Police Station. Everything had to be done from scratch in each district: from identifying the space in the office of the Superintendent of Police (SP) where the Special Cell would function, through appointing the social workers, to training them and creating support systems for them.

Engaging with Discourse and Reform to Address VAW

The Special Cells have always been involved and engaged with the women's movement and wider currents of discourse around VAW. From its very inception, building connections between NGOs and the State systems was a key objective and strategy of the Cell, and this continues to be enshrined in our monitoring indicators. The socio-legal component of the work and processes evolved gradually over the initial years. The monitoring indicators were developed in 2002 during the expansion phase, from our engagement with the police, which needed a framework to supervise the work of Special Cells across Maharashtra.

Throughout the '80s and '90s, the Special Cell built strong referral networks with other women's groups, and we continue to hold and sustain these relationships – drawing on the expertise of women's groups across sectors for our training programmes, building referral networks, and participating actively in the movement and organising.

In 2005, the Protection of Women from Domestic Violence Act was introduced. In the early 2000s, we worked closely with those drafting the Act. The final Act emphasised the need for a coordinated multi-agency response, reflecting the heart of Special Cells' practice.

The roles of service providers and protection officers under the Act were modelled on the work of the Special Cells in Maharashtra, and we worked closely with Lawyer's Collective, MARG and other women's groups to participate in meetings and deliberations around the Act. Anjali Dave worked closely with Indira Jaising of Lawyer's Collective, who was a driving force behind the Act. Indira Jaising travelled across the country holding consultations and understanding practices for addressing domestic violence, and the Special Cell participated actively in these discussions, and advocated for infrastructural support and training for the judiciary and State functionaries for implementing the Act. The Special Cell was thus an integral part of this historic journey and contributed to the genesis of this landmark piece of legislation.

Strategies for Sustaining Growth

From 2002 to 2005, I went from district to district to set up the Special Cells. This was an interesting journey for me. Overall, there was excitement about the expansion, but I also encountered people who were resentful and skeptical. However, despite our difficulties, backing from the police buoyed and sustained us.

The social worker plays a key role in this service to mitigate violence against women. At that time, it was important to handhold the social workers very closely. We undertook intensive training for the social workers. We began with a four-week training module for workers, and then did refresher training, every two-three months. I would constantly visit each district and train the police in those districts. I sought to strengthen both the services of the Cells as well as the environmental support through our training component. The DIG(PAW), who supported our work, conducted a series of training programmes with the police, which helped us gain more legitimacy in their eyes, as well as prepared the ground for services to violated women.

The four-week induction training, which we launched during the expansion phase, is now an integral part of our induction procedure. We bring the social workers from various districts together and train them. Four weeks of training creates a strong bond among the workers. We put into practice values from feminist ideology, like how to create peer learning. Our initial experiments worked. This was the learning we gained through our expansion process. We learnt, in a major way, that social workers are our strength, and we have to invest a lot in them. We began having meetings twice a year, from which regional meetings evolved. Thus, we evolved systems that would help us sustain the personnel, sustain interests, help check the burnout, take care of the persons who are reaching out to the violated woman, and help build their capacities.

We identified our allies and stakeholders within the system as well as outside it. We approached NGOs we knew, along with women's groups and colleges of Social Work in the particular districts. Through them, we were fortunate to identify resourceful and like-minded people, with whom we could work. By reaching out to these multiple stakeholders and bringing them on board, we established a strong support base for the Special Cells. Since we believed in accountability, at the end of the three-year period, we made presentations to these various groups about this journey. That was also a fruitful process. It was these various experiences that made those years so memorable.

When we started the expansion process, we had dreamt of only 40 Cells. I remember sitting in the office of Prabhat Ranjan, then DIG(PAW), and drawing up budget after budget for these 40 Cells – now 40 Cells have become 144. I used to say that my big dream was to see the Special Cells become a State/national scheme – little did I know then that this might one day be close to becoming a reality.

After the expansion in Maharashtra in the early years of the first decade of the new century, we received an invitation from the United Nations Development programme (UNDP) to be part of establishing such services in other States of India. Anjali Dave requested me to lead this work, and I first went to Madhya Pradesh and Haryana to put the wheels in motion. In this kind of work, I have learnt that one has to keep sowing the seeds of the work, not knowing when they might finally germinate. Madhya Pradesh did not work out at that time but Haryana did – the climate was suitable there. But when we started the pilot with NCW again in Madhya Pradesh, we had a history on which to fall back.

The acquaintances we had cultivated then are proving to be allies now. I carried my learnings from Maharashtra to other States. The process of expansion in other States such as Haryana and Gujarat was smoother, and during institutionalisation we were able to establish better systems of monitoring and coordination because of the experience in Maharashtra. We also partnered with Oxfam in Gujarat, Andhra Pradesh, Uttar Pradesh and Odisha – initially implementing pilots funded by Oxfam, and in the second phase, taking on a monitoring role, while partner NGOs implemented the Cells themselves. From this work too, certain seeds took root and some did not – in Gujarat, the Special Cells continue to flourish and grew from 6 Support Centres in 5 districts to 60 Support Centres across all districts of Gujarat. We also took the lead in Gujarat on a different kind of State-based VAW intervention – setting up intervention procedures and training personnel for the 181 Helpline for women.

The Resource Centre for Interventions on Violence Against Women

We social workers are great doers, but we are thinking doers. In the process of doing, we struggle, we learn, we evolve. Putting together the Resource Centre for Interventions on Violence against Women in 2007 was Anjali Dave's idea – and this evolved from and was inspired by the expansion process itself. Through this, we have attempted to formalise all that we have learnt in the process of establishing Special Cells in different places, while recognising that despite the various shades of difference in each location, there is a certain core of services that must remain intact to be true to our mission.

Through the Resource Centre, we have continued to partner the implementation of Special Cells in Maharashtra, in order to remain in touch with the practice and continuously innovate. Alongside this, we have continued to do intervention research that enriches our practice. The Resource Centre also works with many government bodies to advocate institutionalisation of Special Cells, and has supported expansion in other States.

Currently, the expansion to seven new States (Punjab, Madhya Pradesh, Tamil Nadu, Bihar, Meghalaya, Assam and Uttar Pradesh) is being led by the Resource Centre team. Training is another core component of the work at the Resource Centre, which does trainings for judiciary, police officers, Special Cell workers and coordinators, and other stakeholders. The Resource Centre represents a step towards the larger vision of the Special Cell – developing and consolidating years of experience into critical feminist social work praxis for partnership with the state to end VAW.

Partnership with Police: Persistence and Sustained Commitment

We have been fortunate to enjoy a very close relationship with the police system and have never hesitated to engage with them. I used to sit in Prabhat Ranjan's office and draft my letters, working out salaries and money transfers. He mentored me, much in the same way that Anjali Dave did. The police have seen us working very consistently, and with commitment to sustain the quality of work. I met the present Commissioner of Police for Mumbai, Rakesh Maria, in 1991 when he was the Superintendent of Police in Raigad. When he sees me today, he might remember me as a 23-year-old who began working on the issue of violence against women, and who, at 50, is still committed to the same work.

Our strong commitment to the work has earned us respect within the system; without which we would never have been accepted or been able to succeed. Our persistence has paid off. We did have the one-off odd setback, but we never took it to heart. We persisted in our work – the essence of which is to reach the violated woman and empower her to fight her own battles. We are still engaged in this battle, to build recognition for this type of intensely-trained social work intervention within the police system. Although this kind of work is not for everyone, we have taken pride in our work and efforts, and in the kind of backing we continue to have from the police.

Setbacks and Recognition from the Criminal Justice System

A key goal of the Special Cells has been to engage with the state and work with state mechanisms to increase accountability; along with upholding the right of women survivors to self-determination and choice. *Our non-negotiable principles have been that violence under any circumstance is not acceptable and is a crime, and that women have the fundamental right to a life free of violence.* Women require diverse responses to the problem of violence against women, and the location of the Cells within the police systems is an effort towards making the system recognise women's right to choice, and also making the state accountable for supporting them in exercising their choices.

A setback to the mission of the Special Cells came in the form of a government circular issued in 2014 prohibiting 'counselling' of women survivors of violence by service providers appointed under the Protection of Women from Domestic Violence Act 2006 (PWDVA) at police stations, without a court order directing counselling. This was a difficult time, as the circular would have negated decades of work with the State, and contravened the Special Cell's fundamental mission of supporting and upholding rights of survivors to make decisions about their life's path and means of redressal of violence.

However, the Special Cells found support from women's groups in challenging this circular and joined in a PIL seeking to quash it. The process of fighting for our space within the system, and clarifying the nature of our work, was ultimately a valuable one as the final judgment in the case only served to underscore its importance and value. Along with copetitioners Jaya Sagade, Stri Mukti Sangathan, Bharatiya Stree Shakti and Lawyer's Collective, we argued that the circular violates the fundamental right of choice of a woman, who approaches the service providers under the PWDVA, located within the police stations, to choose to access counselling in order to address her problems and individual situation.

Women cannot be forced to address violence through the judicial system alone, and the circular misrepresented the PWDVA which itself mandated the institution of service provider networks to meet the diverse needs of women. We were successful in our suit and the resultant judgment affirmed that 'a violated woman must be entitled to the freedom of choice. It is for her to decide the course of action. It is for NGOs who have the expertise to provide her with advice' (Jaya Sagade v. Maharashtra 2015), along with spelling out the importance of counselling, and the clear differences between counselling and mediation.Thus, the judgment emphasised and highlighted the importance of a specialised feminist approach to counselling survivors, and affirmed the role of the Special Cells in providing services to women under the DV Act. This setback thus resulted in the cocept of Special Cells receiving additional formal backing and recognition from the criminal justice system and has only strengthened our resolve and belief in the work.

New Phase of Growth, and a Vision for the Future

In more recent years, we have found support from new and old partners to realise our dream. We have now expanded to pilots in seven new States across the country with the support of the National Commission for Women as well as State governments and the police. Our key aim continues to be institutionalisation, and working to expand and grow the kinds of services women facing violence can access in institutional spaces. My vision for the Special Cell is evolving into different kinds of multi-agency models to help the woman survivor–working with the police, other components of the criminal justice system (CJS), and the health system. I would also want the Special Cells to have more structure and visibility. I hope for more systematic and structured institutionalisation. Getting recognition for the need for social services within these systems is our larger vision, and I look forward to the journey ahead.

—Trupti Jhaveri Panchal, Project Director
RCI-VAW, Tata Institute of Social Sciences,
Mumbai, January 2019

Review of Debates Around Feminist Interventions on VAW

Women's Movement, Context and Response

VIOLENCE AGAINST WOMEN has become a pandemic social problem in the last two decades in India. The National Family Health Survey (NFHS-3) pegs the prevalence of domestic violence (DV) in India at ranging from 6 per cent to 60 per cent, with considerable variation across the States in different settings (NFHS, 2006). However, other studies emphasise that the magnitude, extent, and gravity of the problem in the country have not been accounted for, as the reporting of the problem is still inadequate (Krishnan, 2005; Koenig et al 2006).

Overall, one-third of women in the age group of 15-49 years have experienced physical violence and about 1 in 10 have experienced sexual violence (NFHS, 2006). In total, 35 per cent have experienced physical or sexual violence. This figure translates into millions of women who have suffered, and continue to suffer, at the hands of husband and other family members (Ibid). According to statistics from around the globe, one out of every three women has experienced violence in intimate relationships at some point in their lives. This is an average based on available national surveys across industrialised and developing countries (WHO, 2007).

Despite its widespread prevalence, this violence has remained largely invisible. Legal jurisprudence has historically considered the 'domain of the house' as within the control and unquestionable authority of the male head of the household; and perceived acts of violence against members of the household, whether wife or child, as discipline, essential for maintaining the rule of authority within the family (ICRW, 1999). It has been observed that even today in the South Asian context, 'A major barrier to needed legal and social reform is the continued lack of recognition that women and girls are first and foremost citizens, individuals who should be accorded the same rights and privileges as men and boys. A perception of women as victims or subjects – rather than as individuals with rights to their own identities, sexualities, and other forms of self-expression – has circumscribed the social and legal provisions for women's safety' (WHO, 2014).

Before the women's movement in the early 1970s, globally, the problem of men's violence against women was viewed as insignificant and attributable mainly to individual – and frequently female – pathology (Thorne-Finch, 1992). In the early 1970s, the women's and battered women's movements identified 'wife beating' as a social problem in the United States and vocalised the need for an expanded public role in identifying and responding to Domestic Violence (DV) (Martin, 1976). It has also been observed in the South Asian context, that a large number of men and women condone violence and believe that it is *normal* and *acceptable* (Solotaroff and Pande, 2014).

In several international conventions, there has been an explicit acknowledgment of the state's responsibility for human rights violations by private actors in both the public and private spheres. The UN Convention on the Elimination of All Forms of Discrimination Against Women (CEDAW) (of which India is a signatory) was a landmark development in 1979, which upheld women's rights; and the Vienna Accord of 1993 and the Beijing Platform of 1995 together crystallised the principle that women's rights are human rights. The frameworks that these conventions established have created a space in which issues like DV, once considered private, came to be understood as human rights violations of public concern. In this way, human rights discourse has started to challenge and erode the public-private divide and has provided a moral momentum for direct response by national governments and non-governmental actors.

The women's movement in India, from the 1980s onwards, has engaged in multiple ways with the issue of violence against women. Ilina Sen notes that post-independence, it increasingly became 'clear that the constitutional promise of equality did not mean much unless basic assumptions regarding equality were challenged'. While having roots in the struggle for independence during the colonial period, as well as in the new social movements and unrest brewing from 1967-1975, the women's movement came into its own during the 1980s and from a largely middle/'upper' caste/class movement, grew to be more cognisant of intersecting identities and oppressions (Burte, 2013). As the movement's understandings of gender and identities have evolved through the years, so too have understandings of and responses to violence against women.

The 1970s were an important time for the women's movement in India, and in 1975 the UN Declaration of a 'Woman's Year' gave it further impetus (Aruna Burte, 2013). In the 1970s, the women's movement identified the high number of 'accidental deaths' and 'kitchen accidents' as a cause for concern, and lobbied successfully for the introduction of specific legislation to address and criminalise marital cruelty as well as dowry death (Jaising, 2009). As Indira Jaising notes, 'the campaign against dowry and related violence in the mid-1970s was, possibly, the first time the issue of violence at home was discussed in public' (Ibid). The result of this campaign was Section 498A of the IPC, which was enacted in 1983 and criminalised marital cruelty making it a non-bailable, non-compoundable offence. The introduction of these amendments criminalised domestic violence for the first time, and highlighted the government's will to combat violence against women even in the private domain. As a result, any cruelty in the form of physical and mental violence inflicted on a woman by her husband and relatives came to be defined as cognisable and punishable offense.

The state of Emergency declared by the then Prime Minister, Indira Gandhi, stifled the burgeoning movements across the country, but the women's movement 'exploded on the Indian political scene after 1977' (Raka Ray, 2000). During the 1980s, with the widespread attention garnered by the custodial rape of Mathura, a young tribal woman, multiple forms of violence faced by women came to the fore. This phase, identified as the 'second wave' of the Indian Women's Movement, brought more educated middle-class women into the public sphere to share their experiences of Domestic Violence (Burte, 2013), and made multiple forms of violence against women a more visible and central concern.

Throughout the 1980s, Indian society witnessed numerous protests by women's organisations against dowry deaths, custodial rape, abductions of women, *sati*, technology used for sex-selection of foetus, sexual harassment of young girls and women in public places, trafficking, and prostitution. The 1980s was also the time when growing discourse around the differing experiences of women from various caste, class and communal locations began to emerge and voice their concerns about the hegemony of the 'upper' caste and class women in the women's movement. As Gopika Solanki and Geethika Gangoli point out, 'the nascent feminist groups emerging in the late 1970s and early 1980s focused primarily on the issues of police and state-initiated violence against women' (Solanki & Gangoli, 2016).

There are similar continued instances of violence against women in this millenium that have broken the public-private binary due to campaigns and protests. This has resulted in a forced confrontation of the state and the country with the reality of VAW in India including the sati of Roop Kanwar, the rape of Bhanwari Devi, the rape and murder of Jyoti Singh in 2012. During the last four decades, the Indian women's movement has thus contributed to a growing public awareness of violence against women. Women activists have mobilised and pressed for significant changes in the criminal code and police procedures in order to address various acts of violence.

With the passing of the Protection of Women from Domestic Violence Act 2005, the public recognition of domestic violence has increased, and there has been an outcry for more effective intervention programmes. This outcry is based on an understanding of the widespread nature of the problem and the incredible costs involved for victims and society as a whole.

Along with the legal reforms came the state's response to violence against women in the form of establishing All Women Police Stations, Family Counselling Centers, Shelter Homes and Family Courts. This marked the beginning of attempts by the state to provide some options outside of the family to women facing domestic violence. However, the insidious, everyday violence experienced by majority of women has remained hidden in the private domain, as *preservation of family* continues to be a primary concern for the state.

Violence, Power and the State

Through years of work, feminist groups have developed and consolidated key guiding principles for working on VAW interventions. They suggest that in the first instance, 'these organisations, through their praxis, see domestic violence as a continuum between mental and physical violence', and also that episodic violence or incidents of violence are not divorced from structural violence, which is socially embedded in structures like *marriage* and *family*. Feminist groups and collectives, therefore, also advocate for laws and services to better address not only marital violence, but all forms of gender-based violence, including violence faced by single women, workplace violence, and violence against queer women.

Solanki and Gangoli point out that 'Indian feminist centres offer a variety of services, ranging from counselling to arbitration, mediation, and adjudication in religious and family laws. They also provide emotional support to women; build counter-hegemonic spaces; enable women to join legal and other feminist campaigns; help them access shelters, medical services and legal aid; intervene with their immediate and extended families, neighbourhoods, caste and sect councils, community leaders and members (including religious organisations and groups); and often arrange for employment and other support through informal networks' (Solanki & Gangoli, 2016). Thus, women's groups, in addition to legal advocacy, adopt a wide range of intervention strategies to help women survivors. The Special Cell, established in 1984, was a part of, and grew with, the Indian Women's Movements.

Intimate Partner Violence (IPV) is one of the most common forms of violence that women experience globally. Violence against women is not a singular event; it is a multi-faceted process, which encompasses acts of mental, physical, sexual as well as financial abuse. Violence is also a manifestation of the assertion of power and authority by a person or institution over a subordinated group or its members. Those who approach violence from a human rights or gender/feminist perspective use the terms 'violence against women' (VAW) or 'gender-based violence' (GBV) to refer to this full domain of abuses. The use of these umbrella terms underscores what all forms of abuse have in common – namely the fundamental devaluation and subordination of women.

Feminist theories of the origins and dynamics of domestic violence have been particularly influential in exposing the issue, campaigning for change, and in sponsoring practical action to address abuse. They draw on the accounts of abused women and an understanding of how patriarchal attitudes, institutions and gendered power differentials have fostered inequality, male privilege, and a sense of male entitlement. Violent behaviour operates as a route to achieving and maintaining male domination, power and control (Eisikovits & Edleson 1989, Hamberger & Hastings 1993, Cunningham et al 1998, Healey et al 1998, Mauricio & Gormley 2001).

The contextualisation of power in the realm of gender dynamics in marital relations involves access to, and control over resources, division of labour, and control over sexuality. Power, therefore, involves the various mechanisms using which these aspects are regulated within the patriarchal milieu. There is thus a need to deconstruct the meanings and connotations of the term 'power' itself, using the feminist lens. Feminists like Rajeswari Sunder Rajan have argued that in the realm of gender, autonomous access to agency is more important than just acquisition of power (Rajan, 2006).

In the late 1990s, Lori L Heise proposed the ecological framework to understand violence against women, which is gaining wider acceptance, and was adopted and consolidated by WHO in 2002. This model locates violence within a layered patriarchal ecology rather than pathologising or individualising violence. It suggests that intimate partner violence does not occur within a vacuum; rather it is rooted within a layered ecosystem of factors that contribute to the violence.

The innermost level is at the level of the individual – and lays out biological or interpersonal factors that contribute to violence. These can also be connected to the partners' own childhood experiences, their learnt relational behaviours, and the relationship patterns they have developed.

Surrounding this are community-based factors, such as social norms in a particular community that normalise and encourage intimate partner violence, gendered community expectations, community structures and power hierarchies, women being located as receptacles of community honour, and stigma for divorce, separation, and violence-challenging behaviours of women. The woman and man's social locations come into play here, with intersections between caste, class and gender – all creating conditions that contribute to violence and conflict. At the macro-social or societal level, wider patriarchal social structures, limited rights and entitlements for women, lack of opportunities and education for women, and discriminatory legal structures, come into play to further entrench Intimate Partner Violence (Heise, 1998).

As Heise points out, ecological thinking represented a significant step forward for the field of violence studies because it conceptualised the causes of violence as probabilistic rather than deterministic. In other words, factors operating at different levels combine to establish the likelihood of abuse occurring. No single factor is sufficient, or even necessary, for partner violence to occur (Heise, 2011). This thus represents a major shift from earlier individualistic formulations of IPV, which located 'causes' for violence within individuals and events.

The ecological model also presents a significant challenge to counselling interventions for violence, as by locating violence as arising from a wider ecology, it thus follows that interventions must engage with the ecology of violence and not just the individual. Feminist activists and theorists have always argued that patriarchy is deeply entrenched in the structure of all state institutions. *The state plays a controlling role in women's lives by operating with a patriarchal bias in its policies and practices,* and ignoring and minimising women's experiences of violence as a 'family matter' and legitimising men's power and use of violence (Michael Hanmer, 1990).

With the understanding that the state plays a vital role in controlling women's lives, it has been argued that it is inappropriate to conceptualise violence on the basis of men's control over women alone. Murphy points at the state's role which says that 'men's violence cannot be understood outside a context' in which case, the state does not intervene to support a woman's apparent right to name such violence as criminal, and in which access to the material means to escape violence in the home is restricted (C Murphy, 2009).

One of the changes feminists sought for women during the 1980s in India and elsewhere was to focus on reforms in laws, so that domestic violence could be recognised as criminal. Section 304B and Section 498A of the Indian Penal Code criminalised the murder of a wife for dowry and marital cruelty respectively, and reflected this concern. Once the legislation was in place, it was crucial to women's safety and survival that the police, lawyers and the courts use the legislation appropriately (J Hanmer et al 1989). However, as MaçKinnon argues, and as it has played out in experience and the nation's courts after the passing of these laws, the law sees and treats women the way men see and treat women (Murphy, 2009).

The reality of this argument continues to reverberate in Indian society still. Even today, in India, domestic violence against women reported to the police is considered low priority, and is colloquially called the 'soft' sector of police work, as the family is seen as sacrosanct, and is to be preserved at any cost – unless the violence is of 'severe' nature. In these cases, women cannot depend on the police system, whose agenda is reconciliation, whereby women are often pushed back into violent relationships.

Feminists like Hanmer have argued that the state is as much part of the problem as the solution (Hanmer, 1990). As women's ongoing experiences show, men's *sense of entitlement to use violence against their partners* contributes to the continuation of domestic violence (Ellen Pence, 1999). It is thus crucial to engage beyond legal reform, to build wider accountability for VAW, and sensitivity and awareness in handling such cases, into the state system and state services.

Feminist Intervention Models for VAW

There is much debate on feminist intervention models for domestic violence; especially when interventions involve counselling, reconciliation, or working with perpetrators and other stakeholders or familial connections of the survivor. The Special Cells emphasise a coordinated, multi-agency feminist response – and in this context, literature on, and responses to, institutional or interventions work with survivors and perpetrators has been briefly reviewed in this section.

The most widely accepted perpetrator education/intervention programme curriculum globally is the Duluth model, a feminist theory paradigm that is based on the premise that violence is used by men in order to control women's behaviour and reinforce male dominance (Van Wormer, 2009). The groundbreaking work of the Duluth Domestic Abuse Intervention Project promotes an integrative approach (Pence & Paymar, 1993). It stresses the use of a coordinated community response involving the cooperation of the criminal justice system, women's shelters and counselling agencies, assaultive men's intervention programmes, community members and other agencies concerned with ending violence against women in relationships.

The Duluth model of community work emphasises on *taking the blame off the woman survivor*, works to facilitate change for the offender, and sets up coordinated community support structures for the survivor to ensure safety and empowerment. The model entails coordination between key stakeholders such as 911 services, shelters, law enforcement, courts, restorative justice circles and counselling/casework programmes for men; with a central monitoring and tracking entity that ensures coordination. Advocates for the Duluth model argue that men will only be held truly accountable for their actions when law enforcement, victim advocates, the courts, and batterer intervention providers coordinate their efforts and services.

Gondolf notes that the cultural climate (actions, values, and procedures of police officers, probation officers, district attorneys and judges) in which a programme operates greatly impacts its effectiveness (EW Gondolf, 2002). It is, thus, also crucial for the criminal justice system to take a strong and unambiguous stand against domestic violence. In this context, Evan Stark makes the case that mandatory arrest policies for perpetrators of domestic violence (relevant in the Indian context, given the non-compoundable non-bailable nature of section 498A) do 'work', because they demonstrate to society that battering is wrong and punishable.

Whether or not the policies work to reduce recidivism in specific batterers, these policies do serve to openly withdraw any consent of the criminal justice system to wife abuse (Stark, 1996). However, Jean Baker Miller found that women did not use their sense of personal power (derived from an independent income) to end domestic violence. Rather, she found that victims' perception of legal power (derived from their satisfaction with the police action taken) could be used to make them feel safer and control their interactions with violent partners in the future. She concluded that 'the most reasonable criminal justice and social service responses to domestic violence are those that consider the victim's needs by taking into account her subjective experiences, her cultural and social resources, and her personal and legal resources' (Miller, 2001). *A successful community response to domestic violence thus needs to establish the means to evaluate state and community interventions from the standpoint of women who are seeking protection and successful intervention to prevent further abuse.*

Feminist approaches to domestic or intimate partner violence, also have to contend with critics citing women's use of violence. Shamita Das Dasgupta suggests that women's violence is not, in fact 'just like men', and that approaches that are quick to decry women using violence against their partners fail to account for the power differentials between the couple. She advocates, instead, for a contextual analysis of women's use of violence, and emphasises that violence is a part of a pattern of coercion, and cannot be looked at as isolated incidents. Two individuals in a conflict do not necessarily possess the same negotiating power – and further, women in violent relationships may not be able to simply walk away and may be drawn deeper into conflict (Dasgupta, 1999). Violence perpetrated by women, as she emphasises, is thus done most often in self-defence, as a means of self-preservation in a violent relationship.

Anti-feminists are quick to claim women's violence, not just on men but on other women, as evidence that gender-specific policy is discriminatory. The debate around Section 498A, a law criminalising marital cruelty in India, is a telling example – where public sentiment as well as the patriarchal biases of the criminal justice system rally to dilute the law and 'protect' the accused from false arrest and 'misuse' of the law (Flavia Agnes, 2015).

In the Indian context, popular discourse around women's use of violence specifically focuses on violence by mothers-in-law against their daughters-in-law. Gangoli and Martin Rew analyse women's use of violence against women in India, and suggest that in some contexts (for example female foeticide, communal violence) this violence comes from self-preservation, whereas in others (taking up arms, participating in communal ideology), it comes from 'prestige they may enjoy as reward for participating in nationalistic and other social movements' (Gangoli & Rew, 2011).

However, violence against daughters-in-law forms a third category, which is currently predominantly routed in popular discourse through dowry violence. Rew and Gangoli point towards the existing joint family structure in India, in which the mother-in-law has almost exclusive control over the deportment of the daughter-in-law, and due to lack of privacy, the couple's relationship develops trouble.

Further, women's power in a patriarchal family setting draws on rewards offered within this space; which may come at the cost of violence against another woman. Gangoli, Rew and

Aisha K Gill thus locate the violence between women-in-law in everyday practices of power and control, and argue that it takes the form of strategic and intentional acts (such as verbal threats and physical violence), as well as culturally and habitually embodied practices (community-based gender role expectations, community monitoring of wives), and that patrilineal inheritance norms also play a role in family dynamics.

Coordinated community work gained traction in the western context, although responses in the west have tended to focus more on shelter provision than they have in the Indian context (Gill Hague, 2013). Hague also points out that while in the western context, emphasis on individualism and its associated socio-cultural dynamics led to an initial emphasis on shelters and individual living for women, Indian responses, on the other hand, have tended to emphasise working more widely with the police or with counsellors to try to change the woman's situation within her community, and to adopt a cultural focus on women's relatedness within families and the value of the (often joint) family in finding solutions to the violence being experienced.

Hague suggests that refuge shelters might not work in contexts where 'the possibly all-embracing embeddedness of extended families and of informal support networks for women, and the difficulty of intervening in such structures and ways of life' may lead to the woman experiencing more difficulties in rebuilding a life outside of these ties (Hague, 2013). *In the Indian context, therefore, there is more emphasis on working with community and familial networks of women, to facilitate and negotiate for an end to violence, and a safe and healthy life within the context of these relationships.*

The issue of conducting joint meetings with men and women is a complex one, and western literature tends to identify such work as dangerous for women. However, advocates of couples' groups (Dunford 2000a & b) argue that it can be empowering for the woman to witness her abuser being challenged by authority figures, and that the presence of women in a group can reduce victim blaming and make role play more realistic.

Other conjoint therapy practitioners maintain that in the absence of clear evidence for the superiority of other forms of domestic violence intervention, couples' therapy specifically geared to addressing physical and psychological aggression is a valid approach, providing it has been ascertained that the violence is not severe and the woman is not in fear of her partner. Indian feminist groups have and continue to conduct joint work, with the belief that the woman's safety and self-determination be kept at the forefront of the intervention.

Sangeeta Rege and Aarthi Chandrashekhar in their review of 22 women's groups, found that of the groups that do direct interventions work with women, do joint work with couples as well, if the woman wishes to engage with the violent partner to work toward ending the abuse. All of these groups articulate feminist politics and values, and believe that working to change violent men is a part of their feminist politics. As these two scholars point out, 'one of their biggest challenges in enabling women to deal with violence, has been that most women want to continue with the relationship but want the violence to stop. Most organisations have responded to this need by adopting the method of joint meetings with the abuser to negotiate for non-violence, though many counsellors admit that such a change in the behaviour of the abuser is only temporary in nature' (Rege & Chandrasekhar, 2013).

Padma Bhate-Deosthali in her narrative of the journey of setting guidelines for hospital-based crisis counselling centres, Dilaasa, writes that joint meetings 'are used as a method to create a non-violent space in which women can engage in dialogue with their abusers and the family members, to negotiate for cessation of violence and receive an assurance of their safety'. These are arranged when the woman desires them, and before they are conducted, extensive preparatory work is done with the woman. The counsellor will, during the meeting, facilitate and help the woman articulate her demand for non-violence (Deosthali, 2015).

Ramesh Awasthi argues, in fact, that domestic violence be considered by interventionists as a 'kinship' concern. Most women first turn to community and kinship networks for support, and negotiations within these networks are rarely undertaken from a women's rights perspective. Thus, as feminist interventionists, it is important to engage with these structures to bring about negotiation from the woman's perspective, and emphasise her right to health and a violence-free home (Awasthi, 2013).

Rege points towards the potential pitfalls of working with men. She suggests that the power imbalance in the counselling relationship between the client and the counsellor, can lead to the counsellor being perceived as a 'superior person' by the client, who can solve all her problems. This leads to dependency on the part of the client, but also leads to expectations that the counsellor will exert power to 'punish' or discipline the perpetrator for the violence, which will lead to an end of the abuse.

Interventionists who work with men must, therefore, navigate these expectations, and focus not on mediating between a couple, but on facilitating the woman's voice and assertion. Rege also warns that a 'goal dissonance' between the counsellor and client, when the client wishes to return to a potentially violent home or relationship, should also be analysed from the perspective of power imbalance, as the counsellors must listen carefully to the women and ensure that they do not use their power to influence a victim woman's decision-making. She writes that 'in order to truly share power, the counsellor has to set a goal in conjunction with the client's expectations and encourage her to assess her own safety, vis-à-vis the current situation and make suggestions towards intervention techniques to prevent further abuse as well as providing practical survival tips to seek support from others' (Rege, 2013).

In the Indian context, Bhate-Deosthali, Rege and Prakash's volume on *Feminist Counselling and Domestic Violence in India* provides valuable insight into how the women's movement and feminist groups in India have worked to tackle violence and domestic abuse. In this volume, Rajani Gupte locates the value of using the feminist lens in domestic violence interventions. She cites the history of the women's movement and identifies feminism as a movement for rights-based gender equality. Gupte thus suggests that feminism is intrinsically about challenging power. Feminism also comes from multiple social locations and perspectives. This challenge to patriarchal power is crucial to locate within the counselling paradigm.

The women's movement in India has placed clear emphasis on the fact that domestic violence is not a 'private' matter – drawing directly from the feminist slogan of 'the personal is political'. By politicising the issue of violence and refusing to address domestic violence as a set of isolated incidents, the movement paved the way for VAW interventions to also identify themselves politically, and locate and challenge patriarchal power through counselling or casework.

Gupte also points towards the context of domestic violence counselling that existed in India before 2010, where 'family counselling', which pushed for reconciliation and 'compromise' as the goal was the norm. The women's movement challenged such work, and sought to set up alternative paradigms where the woman's agency and needs were placed at the centre of the intervention, rather than the goal of 'saving the family' (Gupte 73). Gupte writes that 'just as absence of illness does not amount to being considered healthy, the mere absence of violence does not indicate an equal relationship between men and women' – signaling that the fundamental commitment of feminist counselling is not just superficial problem-solving, but in-depth empowerment work with clients.

Feminist counselling initially defined itself against traditional 'phallocentric' and patriarchal approaches, which were rooted in essentialist gender differences and encouraged women to 'adjust to their life circumstances' (Nayan Joshi, 2013). Gradually, in the western context, more specific articulations of feminist counselling practice began to emerge post the 1980s (Joshi 2013). However, as Joshi points out, in its earlier stages, the women's movement in India did not have close ties with the field of mental health, and even today there are fewer scholarly articulations of feminist mental health practice for domestic violence.

Undurthi Vindhya argues that *while feminism seeks to address broader social change, counselling is as valuable to the feminist movement as advocacy, and can be as political.* She writes that feminist counselling, challenging the dominant psychological model which encourages women to 'adjust', first validates women's voices and experiences and acceptance of the client. Empowerment is a key component of these interventions, where the client is actively involved in developing solutions. Importantly, Vindhya sees feminist counselling as a part of 'consciousness-raising', whereby the client's individual problems are viewed through the wider feminist lens, located within broader structures of violence and inequality, and the client is helped by the counsellor in connecting her experiences to feminist understandings of power and control.

The Special Cell for Women

The 'Special Cell for Women' approach was first developed and demonstrated in Maharashtra in 1986. Drawing from the belief that violence against women is a crime against society and that the state must take responsibility for addressing it, the Special Cell placed two trained social workers in police stations, to provide psycho-socio-legal support to women facing violence and seeking state support.

Over the years, the Special Cells have expanded to 14 States with over 30 years of work with the criminal justice system. As Anjali Dave writes, 'The location of the Special Cells within the police system is of crucial significance. In a country where the state espouses to be a welfare state, social services continue to remain minimal and not yet a right. Women in vulnerable situations are further marginalised by their communities and families, especially when hierarchies and subjugations are contested. In this context, the police service is one of the only agencies available at all times, free to begin with, and constitutionally bound to protect its citizens from violence and crime' (Dave, 2013). Thus, the Special Cells synthesise their strategic location with a pro-woman, feminist perspective, in their work with survivors of violence.

The Mission Statement and Monitoring Indicators of the Special Cells articulate the key thrust of their interventions work. Locating its strategic thrust as working at both the individual and systemic level to bring visibility to the voices of women survivors of violence, engage in problem-solving and build a coordinated multi-agency response to violence against women, the documents go on to discuss the key working principles of the Special Cell.

The first indicator emphasises 'social work interventions for providing emotional support and strengthening the psychological self of the violated woman', locating this as the guiding principle. Thus the Cell works to empower women, connect their experiences to the wider framework of patriarchal inequity, and takes a rights-based approach to the violence they are facing (TISS, 2016).

The Special Cells articulate a pro-woman approach, which entails that the woman and her needs are kept at the centre of the interventions process. Thus, if the woman so requires, after individual work, safety planning and needs assessment, for intervention with her partner, the Special Cell conducts joint meetings as well as individual meetings with the violent man, to work towards ending violence and behaviour change. Thus, while prioritising the safety needs of the woman facing violence, the Special Cell does, on a case-to-case basis, undertake feminist social work interventions with violent men. Data and research on the Special Cells over the years have reflected the value of working with men, families, and the state in ending violence.

The first evaluation of the Special Cell (2004), in assessing client expectations and satisfaction, found that non-violent reconciliation with their partner was an expectation of 61.7% of the women interviewed. The other 33% were clear that the relationship will not work and though needed help did not expect reconciliation, of which 19.5% wanted divorce and 6.3% wanted separation from their partner.

As many as 75.2% of women expressed the feeling that intervention with husband would help solve their problem. In keeping with this, the social workers carried out interventions work with partners for 73.6% of women. For this, it became crucial that the Special Cell does empowerment work with women and works with the perpetrator of violence, to bring about substantive change in the woman's circumstances and environment.

A majority of women (77.9%) reported physical violence, 82.5% reported mental harassment, and 72.3% reported non-fulfillment of roles and responsibilities by their husband – these together comprised the majority of abuse that women faced. However, a significant portion of women also faced mental harassment by the marital family (62%) and physical violence from in-laws (36.3%). Women largely had a positive response to the Cell's interventions. A majority of women shared that what they liked about the intervention was the Cell worker's approach to problem-solving, and the fact that they felt someone was with them to support them. Women reported increased confidence and control over their emotions as one of the major outcomes of the intervention. Largely, women's responses reflected that the empowerment work done by the worker and the pro-woman approach adopted, was what helped them the most (Vidya Apte, 2004).

Other literature from the Special Cells also reflect women's desire for change in their partners' behaviour. A study on non-cohabiting, non-marital intimate relationships found that in these 'love relationships', women faced more economic and sexual violence than physical violence.Often because of the nature of these relationships and the stigma in India surrounding 'love' relationships and marriages, women felt more helpless and without support, due to the choices they had made in defending their relationship to their family and community.

This also explains the fact that when these women approached the Special Cell, more often than not it was for reconciliation, as they 'fear that their "honour" would be at stake if the relationship does not culminate in marriage' (Dave, Pradhan and Sriraman, 2016). Many of the women in 'love relationships' who approached the Special Cells also reported sexual violence (75%). Thus, keeping the women's empowerment at the centre of the intervention process, the Special Cells have to also work with the partners of these women to facilitate an end to violence.

Violated women approaching an institution like the Special Cell have often been facing violence for many years, and their decision to approach the Special Cell is precipitated or prompted by a specific experience, incident, or feeling. The Special Cell's data on these 'precipitating factors' reveal that the most commonly-cited reason for making a decision to seek the help of the Special Cell was a threat to her resources, and more specifically, dispossession from the marital home (RCI-VAW 2016, internal document). Thus, coupled with data on women's expectations, we see that working to empower women and helping them negotiate for an end to violence, is a crucial component of feminist social work VAW interventions.

In conclusion, we see that the context of violence against women in India, along with state and civil society responses, has evolved considerably since early theoretical models for interventions work with women survivors of violence. The Special Cell for Women and Children, rooted in the women's movement, reflects a form of coordinated multi-agency response to violence against women – prioritising a rights-based pro-woman approach to domestic violence. This document thus seeks to consolidate these practices, through a review of the work and history of this interventions work, with an emphasis on the development of feminist social work praxis at the Special Cell.

Parts of this chapter have been adapted from the author's work: Panchal T J (2017). *Men, intimate partner violence and change: Feminist social work interventions in the Special Cell.* PhD Thesis submitted in fulfillment of the requirements for the Degree of Doctor of Philosophy in Social Sciences, Tata Institute of Social Sciences, Mumbai.

Trends in Data from the Special Cells, 2003-2012

THE PERIOD, FROM 2003 to 2012, was critical in the history of the Special Cell, because the first major burst of expansion occurred during this time. This chapter thus seeks to:

- Analyse trends with regard to clients accessing the Special Cells from the reports of the Special Cells and construct a profile of the violated women who approach the Special Cells for assistance
- Understand the nature of the problems with which the women approach the Special Cells
- Document the problem-solving attempts of the women prior to reaching the Special Cells, and the details of interventions reported by the Special Cell social workers; and
- Compare the trends from the decade of study with the trends from previous periods.

Each Special Cell submits monthly and quarterly reports to TISS (details of this are presented in Annexure 5).

Data from the quarterly reports of all the Special Cells implemented directly by TISS are compiled into six-monthly reports and are circulated to officials in the DWCD at State and district offices, the Home Department, Superintendents of Police at the District Headquarters where the Special Cells are based, the State Women's Commission and the DIG (PAW).

Analysing the data available from these reports provides valuable insights about the women who seek assistance from the Special Cell, as well as about the services and interventions delivered by the Cell social workers. Reviewing this data, we are able not only to construct a demographic profile of the women survivors, but also understand their needs and expectations from this State-based service, and what the service was able to deliver.

For this chapter, we compiled *data from quarterly reports filed by Special Cell workers of 13 of the 14 TISS-implemented Cells for the years 2003 to 2012*. The Special Cell at Vakola, Mumbai became operational in December 2012 and, therefore, has not been included in this study. The resultant dataset contains aggregated data of about 17,962 clients from these 13 Special Cells.

Table 1 presents brief descriptions of the 13 TISS-implemented Special Cells from which data was collected for this report, in order to contextualise the findings.

Quantitative data for each reporting indicator in the quarterly reports was entered in Microsoft Excel by quarter. The different indicators were summed into annual figures. Tables and graphs were generated to understand trends by year and, where possible, by location. We compared the present findings with the findings from the three earlier studies on the Special Cells – *Special Cell for Women and Children* (1994), Anjali Dave and Gopika Solanki (2001) and Vidya Apte (2004), in order to compare the trends of this period with those of the preceeding decades.

Table 1: The 13 TISS Special Cells till 2012

Special Cell	Estd	Notes on demographic composition
Police Commissioner's office at Crawford Market, Mumbai	1984	Urban, very heterogeneous population in terms of religion, language, class
Dadar police station, Mumbai	1988	Urban, mostly lower middle-class population
Kandivali police station, Mumbai	1994	Urban, heterogeneous population in terms of language, class
CBD Belapur police station, Mumbai	2001	Urban, heterogeneous population in terms of language, class, caste, religion
Office of Superintendent of Police, Nanded	2002	Rural and urban population, heterogeneous in terms of class, religion and language, larger proportion of Muslim clients compared to other Cells
Office of Superintendent of Police, Aurangabad	2002	Rural and urban population, heterogeneous in terms of class, mostly Marathi population
Office of Superintendent of Police, Pune	2002	Rural and urban population, heterogeneous in terms of class, mostly Marathi population
Office of Superintendent of Police, Yavatmal	2002	Rural and urban population, heterogeneous in terms of class, mostly Marathi population
Office of Superintendent of Police, Nasik	2003	Rural and urban population, heterogeneous in terms of religion, class and language
Office of Superintendent of Police, Wardha	2003	Rural and urban population, heterogeneous in terms of class, mostly Marathi population
Kurla police station, Mumbai	2010	Urban population, larger proportion of Muslim clients compared to other Cells, mostly economically disadvantaged and lower middle-class population
Vikroli police station, Mumbai	2010	Urban, mostly middle and lower middle-class population, heterogeneous in terms of religion
Dhule, Maharashtra	2011	Rural and urban population, heterogeneous in terms of class, mostly Marathi population

Over the course of writing, we presented our findings to workers and coordinators of the Special Cells. In particular, we tried to understand trends from the data alongside the reported experience of the social workers. The ensuing discussion also informed our analysis, and their insights from the field and interpretations of trends have also been included, in some cases, alongside the data. We also undertook observational visits to Special Cells in Mumbai to gain insight in interpreting the data.

Growing Client Volume and Reach of the Service: A Case for Expansion

While working directly with communities, it is important to be alert to how the service provision is perceived by community members and ensure that it is reaching those who need it the most. A key question for any programme planner is whether there is a felt need for such a programme, and a key metric for evaluation becomes the extent of usage of the service. Over the years, documentation practices, for the purpose of assisting interventions, have come to classify people who first approach the Special Cell in one of two ways: One-time interventions, and new registered clients.

One-Time Interventions refer to clients who visit a Special Cell just once. Such clients often approach the Cell to gather or confirm information about the services of the Special Cells, or its location and procedures; inquire about services of other agencies such as shelters or hostels, or to seek letters of referrals to such support systems; seek clarification related to civil or criminal legal procedures and police procedures; seek direct help for registering non-cognisable or cognisable complaints with the police; or seek pre-litigation advice.

Some such clients make enquiries pertaining to their own circumstances, while others make enquiries on behalf of other people. Such individuals may not need a long-term engagement with the Cell, or if they need it, they may not be ready at that point in time to enter into a long-term engagement. However, though this client is present for a brief period of time, the intervention is by no means superficial: a lot of intense work may take place during this single interaction. These interactions have even been described as crisis interventions.

New Registered Clients are those individuals who have registered their cases in a Special Cell in that year – that is, they enter into a formal process, wherein they write a detailed application describing their reason for seeking help from the Special Cells and continue their engagement with the service to seek a variety of socio-legal services.

Table 2 shows that there were a total of 27,955 one-time interventions across the ten-year period. It is also evident that such cases are increasing over the years from an average of 136.4 clients per Cell in the year 2003 to 343.1 in 2012.

This data also reveals that there were a total of 17,962 registered clients at the 13 Special Cells, with an increase from the average 117.3 clients per Cell in the year 2003 to 203.6 in 2012. Thus, in sum, 26 workers from 13 Special Cells have been able to reach 45,961 women over this ten-year period.

The generally increasing trend in the average number of one-time as well as new registered clients, is an indicator of the growing awareness in the community of the services of the Special Cells. The years 2008 and 2009 show a spike in the average number of new registered clients as well as in the average number of one-time interventions. This appears to be *largely driven by the Special Cell at Nasik, which, according to reports by the local Cell workers, was under the supervision of a highly-motivated police official who created many opportunities for those Cell workers to undertake awareness sessions in the communities.*

Table 2: Number of clients intervened in the Special Cells

Year	Special Cells Reporting	Total One-time Interventions	Average No. of One-time Interventions per Cell	Total New Registered Clients	Average No. of New Registered Clients per Cell
2003	10	1,364	136.4	1,173	117.3
2004	10	1,483	148.3	1,249	124.9
2005	10	1,774	177.4	1,324	132.4
2006	10	2,712	271.2	1,525	152.5
2007	10	2,878	287.8	1,691	169.1
2008	10	3,449	344.9	1,929	192.9
2009	10	2,770	277	2,053	205.3
2010	11	3,071	279.2	2,070	188.2
2011	13	3,994	307.2	2,301	177.0
2012	13	4,460	343.1	2,647	203.6
		27,955		17,962	

Note: 2010 includes data from Kurla Cell; 2011 and 2012 includes data from Vikhroli,Dhule and Kurla Cells

Anecdotally, social workers report that a high percentage of persons seeking one-time help do return to the Cell to register their complaint there. This is often treated by social workers as a sign of the trust they were able to engender in the client. Current reporting systems do not track this percentage or the time interval between persons registering themselves after their initial foray to the Cell. However, from a feminist perspective, the initially hesitant attitude is understandable, given the damaged trust among women survivors.

Further, as we report in the next chapter, many survivors of violence report having sought assistance before they come to the Cell. It is likely that their previous attempts at problem-solving were not helpful and this probably contributes to their lowered expectations from the system.

Effect of addition of new Special Cells on client volume— Our records also give us a sense of the time that it takes for a new Cell to establish itself within the community. The year 2010 saw the addition of two Cells at Vikhroli and Kurla respectively. In 2011, TISS was requested by the Maharashtra government to take over the running of the Special Cell at Dhule due to irregularities detected in the operations of the previous implementing organisation.

Data from three months of functioning of the Kurla Cell was incorporated into the overall database from the year 2010. Vikhroli Cell became operational only in December. Therefore, its data was available only from 2011. **Table 3** presents the total number of new registered clients as well as those receiving only a one-time intervention for these three Cells. Women start approaching a Cell as soon as a Cell is established; and within three years of becoming operational, the Kurla Cell appears to have as much of a case-load as the older Cells.

Table 3: Number of interventions in the Special Cells at Kurla, Vikhroli and Dhule

Year	No. of One-time Interactions			No. of New Registered Clients		
	Kurla	Vikhroli	Dhule	Kurla	Vikhroli	Dhule
2010	25	-	-	14	-	-
2011	122	272	307	108	165	96
2012	284	345	315	121	179	140

Examining the records also shows how the establishment of new Cells affects the client volume in other Cells. If we isolate and remove the number of cases handled by the three new Cells from the annual totals for the Cells for those three years, we see a slight dip in the average number of new registered cases for those years, though the number of one-time interventions continues to rise unabated (**Figure 3** and **Table 4**). We speculate that establishing two new Cells in Mumbai might have resulted in an improved coverage network of services in the city whereby women who come in for initial inquiries at the older Cells may have been referred to Special Cells closer to their homes for registration. As at the time of this analysis in 2012, there were no digital data recording systems that permitted tracking women across Cells, we are unable to support this hypothesis with data.

Apart from the women who approach the Special Cell for help in a particular month, there are also a number of ongoing clients in every active Special Cell. These are clients who have registered applications with the Cell earlier and who continue to access the Cell for intervention across a particular quarter. The Special Cell believes in working at the client's pace, and that a case is never 'closed'. The issues that women survivors face are generally too complicated to be resolved in a short span of

Figure 3: Number of interventions in Special Cells (minus Kurla, Vikhroli and Dhule)

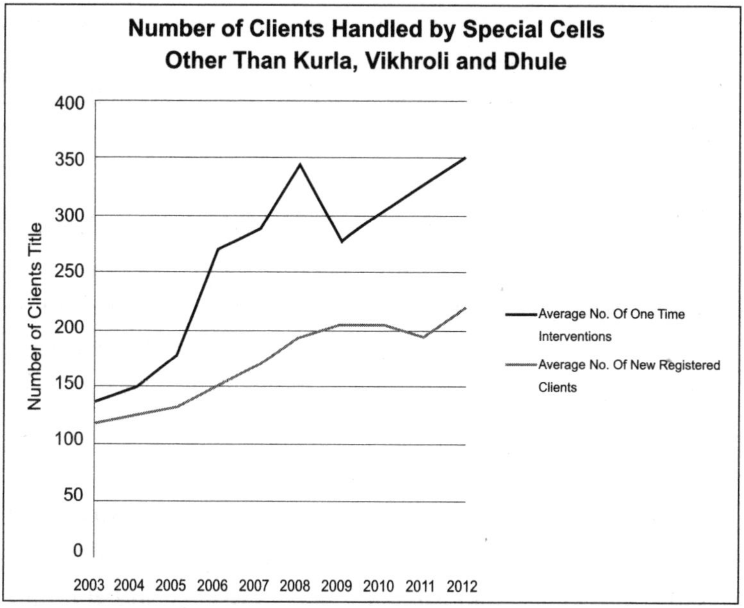

Table 4: Interventions in Cells other than Kurla, Vikroli and Dhule

Year	Special Cells Reporting	Total One-time Interventions	Average No. of One-time Interventions	Total New Registered Clients	Average No. of New Registered Clients
2003	10	1,364	136.4	1,173	117.3
2004	10	1,483	148.3	1,249	124.9
2005	10	1,774	177.4	1,324	132.4
2006	10	2,712	271.2	1,525	152.5
2007	10	2,878	287.8	1,691	169.1
2008	10	3,449	344.9	1,929	192.9
2009	10	2,770	277	2,053	205.3
2010	10	3,046	304.6	2,056	205.6
2011	10	3,293	329.3	1,932	193.2
2012	10	3,516	351.6	2,207	220.7

time. Moreover, the intervention at the Special Cell focuses not only on resolution of the immediate crisis faced by the violated woman, but equally on the long-term development and self-determination of the woman.

The long-term goal of the Special Cells' intervention is to empower every client who reaches the Cell. The intervention process at a Special Cell is, therefore, a long-term process and the number of ongoing cases is considerable. The reporting framework until 2012, however, does not permit us to comment on the average amount of time taken to assist a woman and bring resolution to her immediate needs and her long-term needs.

In conclusion, we see that over the ten-year period, there were a total of 27,955 one-time interventions. There was an increase in the average number of clients per Cell from 136.4 in the year 2003 to 343.1 in 2012. There were 17,962 registered clients at the 13 Special Cells over the ten-year period. There was an increase from an average 117.3 newly registered clients per Cell in 2003 to 203.6 in 2012. This growth in utilisation reflects, therefore, the acceptance that Special Cells have gained within the police system and the community, as well as the felt need for such services. It also serves as strong ground for the Maharashtra government's decision to expand the programme from district level to the taluk level.

A Profile of the Clients at the Special Cells

In this section, we attempt to become more closely acquainted with clients who access the services of the Special Cells, and compare these findings to findings from previous analyses of the records from the Special Cells. Understanding the profile of clients provides insight into the reach of services, as well as in consolidating our understanding of women's experiences of violence in context of their social locations.

GENDER

As expected of such a service, our data shows that the overwhelming majority of clients at the Special Cells were women – 87% (**Figure** 4). However, the number of men who approached the Cells is also sizable (12%). It is, therefore, interesting to unpack the patterns in men accessing these services. Through analysis of the data, it was found that some of these men were fathers or brothers of women facing violence, who register complaints about the abuse meted out to their daughters or sisters (5%).

However, many of these cases were of men with grievances against women (7%). The Special Cell, though primarily a service for women, does register complaints of men regarding their own harassment as this may serve as an entry point to reach the woman in the relationship who may have a greater need of assistance than the man.

Figure 4: Majority of clients at the Special Cells were women

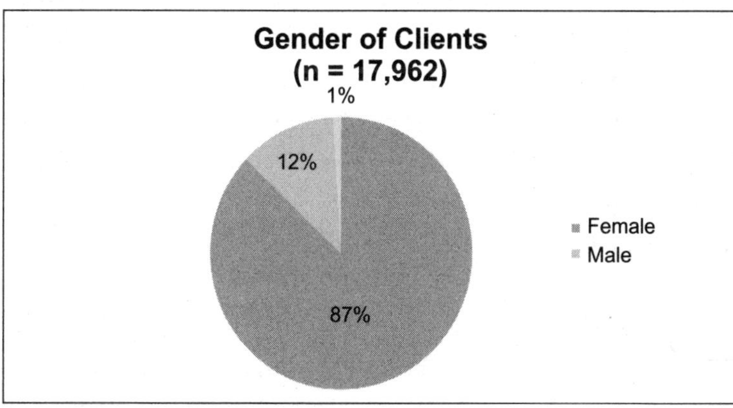

We looked at the change over the last ten years in the proportion of male and female clients. (**Figure** 5). We generated running averages by averaging all past data points as well as the then current data point (in 2012) in order to smooth out outlier figures in our data and to produce more easily recognisable trend lines. The increase in the number of cases of both male and female clients is evident from the graph.

Figure 5: Gender-wise distribution of clients: Year-wise trends

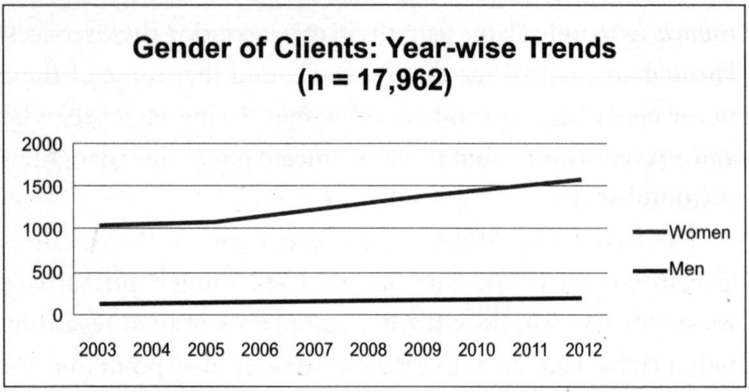

Data from the reports show that often husbands register complaints against their wives on grounds of harassment, desertion, abuse of children or relationship outside marriage (included in **Table 5**). Anecdotal reports from Special Cells' social workers reveal that often in such cases the woman in question is the victim of violence and not the perpetrator. For instance, when men register complaints of harassment and desertion by wife, the workers often find that the wife is forced to leave the house because of violence perpetrated on her. Some complaints of relationships outside marriage are later revealed to be a product of the excessively suspicious nature of the husband. The worker in such cases, targets her interventions to assist the woman, even though the complainant is the male partner. *At the Special Cells, irrespective of who registers the complaint, the intervention is always pro-woman.*

Observations from social workers in the Special Cells also reveal that men who abuse may register such complaints when they feel that their female partner is on the verge of reporting abuse within the relationship to an outside party. Their expectation is that such a step would skew the result in their favour. This is once again an abuse of power by men over women. Special Cells' social workers also report that *when abused women lodge court cases against their husbands, the husbands in question are increasingly advised by their lawyers to register a case in the Special Cell in order to show their willingness to reconcile and strengthen their case in court.* We speculate that the rise in the number of cases registered by men over the years could be a result of this phenomenon.

Since the overwhelming majority of the clients are women, we report our data as generally descriptive of women clients, rather than utilising the more 'neutral' he/she.

Our data shows only one case of a transgender client in the analysis period. Anecdotal reports from the Special Cells reveal that the number may actually be higher, but trans-clients are registered in records not as 'third gender' but as the gender they identify with (In the case of the Special Cell, most often as a woman). One report from Cell workers suggested that most such clients tend to report abuse from their intimate live-in partners.

AGE

Given the nature of the data (compiled six-monthly reports of the Special Cells), it was impossible to disaggregate information regarding age and education of male and female clients of the Special Cells.

With regard to age, we undertook three types of analyses. We sought to understand the age distribution of clients, trends in the age distribution over the ten-year period, and how the age distribution compares to data from previous decades.

Age distribution: In **Figure 6** we present the age distribution of the clients as reported in the quarterly reports. The figure shows that though women of all age groups are susceptible to violence, the largest group of clients (42%) were in the age group of 25 to 34 years. Clients in the age group of 18 to 24 also make up a sizeable segment (30%). Together these groups comprise the reproductive age group. As seen in other studies, this age group tends to be more vulnerable to violence.

There is a small numbers of clients below the age of 18 as well. Unfortunately, quarterly reports do not make clear what, if any, are the specific issues of this age group, though *social workers report that many of these cases are of child sexual abuse.*

Given that domestic violence often begins early within a relationship, why then does our data feature more women between the age of 25 to 34 years? It is possible that women who experience violence take some time to arrive at a decision to seek outside help. Possible hindrances could be stigma attached to such an action, uncertainty of outcome or fear of backlash from the abuser. It is also possible that there may be more restrictions placed on younger women, especially immediately after marriage, which constrict the possibility of contacting an outside party for help.

Older women, namely those in the age group of 25 to 34, may also have more awareness and courage to seek outside intervention than a younger woman in the age group of 18-24 years. At least in the case of some older women, the presence of children may play a critical role: children may bring forth a fresh perspective and questioning of violence, or if also made to endure violence, could serve as tipping points for women to reach out for help.

Our data show that violence continues even in the older age group of 45 and beyond. Anecdotal evidence shows that most of these survivors face violence from their own children. As per a study on the implementation of PWDVA by Monica Sakhrani and Trupti Panchal (2014), often elderly women litigants are widows who were subjected to emotional abuse, deprivation of maintenance or property disputes.

Figure 6: Age of clients

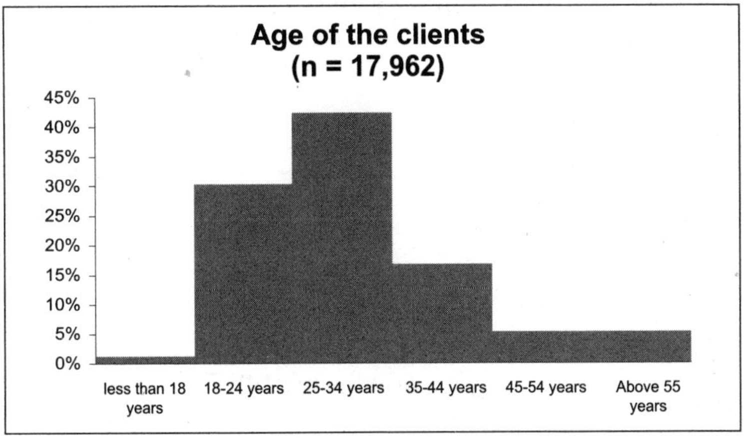

Trends in age distribution

To understand changes in the age composition of our client group across the years, we plotted the age-wise groups by year (**Figure** 7). The most visible year-wise increase in the number of clients coming to the Special Cells occurs in the age group of 25 to 34 years.

The age groups of 18 to 24 years and 35 to 44 years also appear to have registered an increase, but the number of clients in the age groups of less than 18 years and above 45 years has remained more or less the same. That is, the numbers of children, adolescents and senior citizens approaching the Special Cells have remained steady but not increased. This could be due to an increased perception in the community that the Special Cells largely cater to issues of domestic violence among women.

Also, it is possible that there is an increase in specialised service provision for these particular age groups, which means that would-be clients now have more options.

Figure 7: Age of clients: Year-wise trends

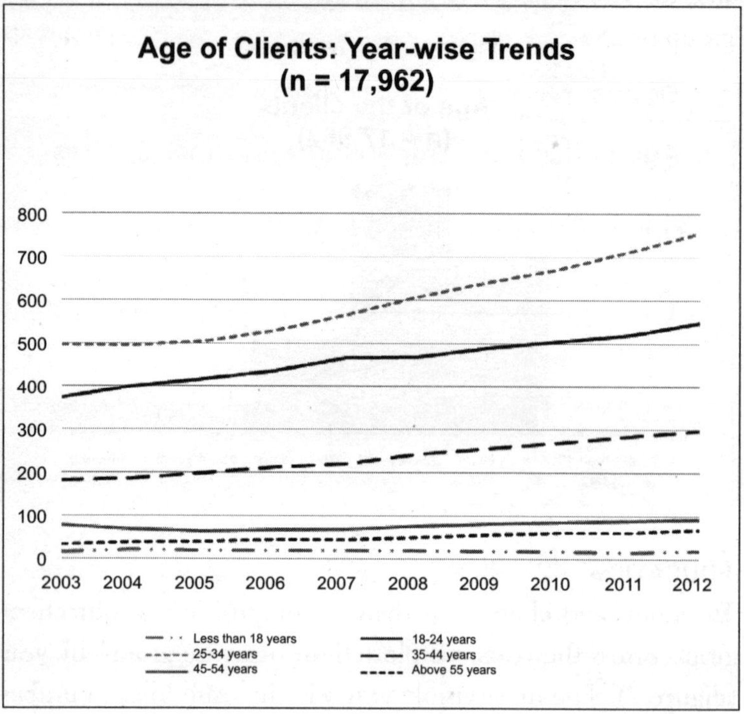

Comparison With Previous Decades

Given that we have studied the same client group in previous years, we sought to understand how the client profile has changed as the programme has expanded. For this, we plotted the age-break up from the current analysis against those reported in the previous studies of the Special Cells.

Our first observation was that the percentage of cases in which the information about age was not available, has steadily reduced from 32% in the 1994 study to 1% in the 2003-2012 analysis. This clearly indicated that the documentation process has significantly improved in the Special Cells.

It is apparent from **Figure 8**, that the age profile of clients in the current review matches the age profile of clients in earlier studies. The majority of clients are consistently from the age group of 25 to 34 years.

Figure 8: Age of Clients: Comparison with Earlier Studies

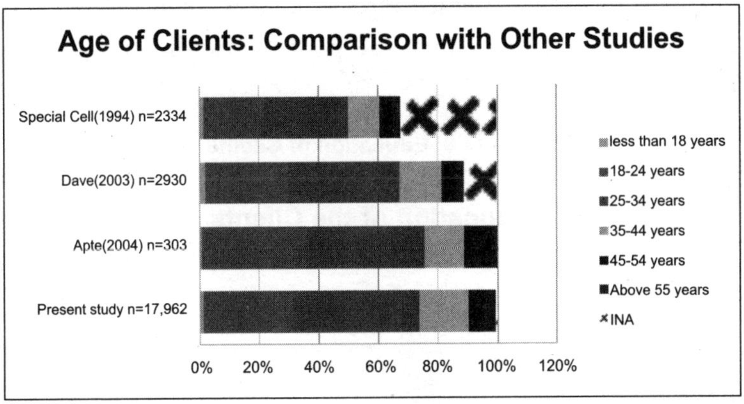

EDUCATION

We undertook similar analysis of educational qualifications of clients, to understand trends across the years, and whether changes across the decades are visible. We found that a majority of clients had some amount of schooling, around 18% reported higher education. *These educational profiles contradict the popular societal belief that VAW is an issue affecting only non-educated sections of the society.*

Distribution of Educational Background

In **Figure 9** we present the educational background of clients as reported in the quarterly reports. It appears that almost a quarter of women (23%) report functional literacy, indicating that the service reaches out successfully to persons of limited privilege. Additionally, 42% of the women who come to the Special Cells have had some amount of schooling and another 18% report higher education including graduation and professional education. The number of non-literate women seeking help against violence is comparatively low (12%). This might be reflective of the literacy attainment of women in the State of Maharashtra in general, as the State does report higher literacy rates among women (75.87% as per 2011 census) and thus the pool of non-literate persons is reducing.

Figure 9: Education of Clients

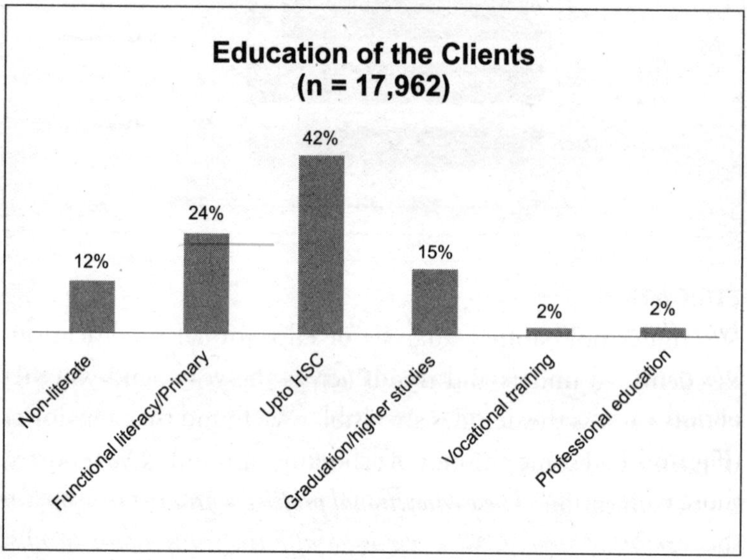

Distribution of Educational Background

We sought to understand the changes in the education level of clients of the Special Cells over the ten years. **Figure 10** shows the running averages. There appears to be a very slight increase in the number of women with professional or higher education who have accessed the services of the Cell over the years. The increase in women graduates appears to be more pronounced. The maximum increase appears to be among women with secondary and higher secondary education. This might reflect both the increasing educational attainment among women in the State as well as greater awareness of the services of the Special Cells.

Figure 10: Education of clients: Year-wise trends

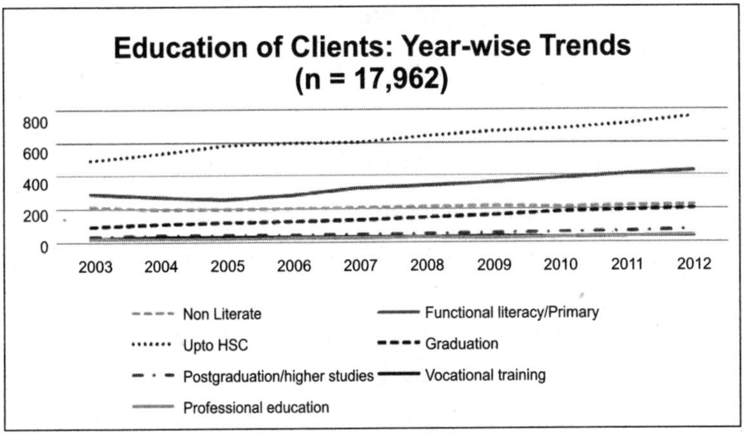

Distribution of Educational Background

We contrasted the educational profile of clients in the current period of analysis with those reported in the earlier studies (**Figure 11**). It appears that women with functional literacy and those with secondary and higher secondary education comprise the majority of clients approaching the Special Cells. The number of non-literate clients approaching the Special Cells is consistently low across all studies. Dave (2001) speculated this could be due to the fact that *in their struggle for daily survival, there is no space for these non-literate women to seek redressal for violence.* The relative proportion of women completing graduation/higher education seems to have increased in studies covering the later time periods.

Figure 11: Education of clients: Comparison with earlier studies

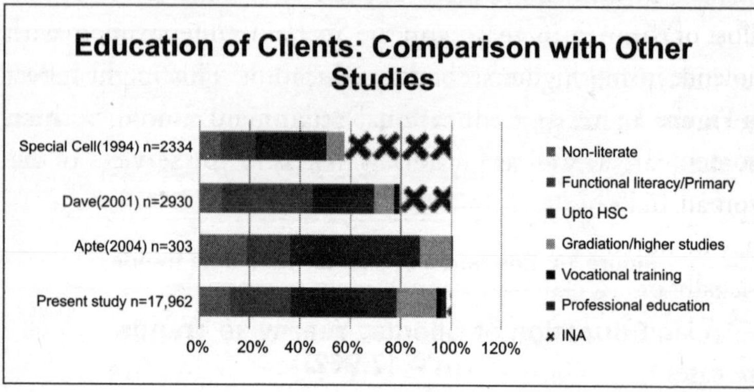

Reasons for Approaching the Special Cells

There is a very wide range of problems with which women approach the Special Cells. We present these issues in the following broad categories:

- Violence with husband/marital family as the perpetrator
- Cases registered by husbands
- Violence in non-marital intimate partner relationship
- Domestic violence other than marital/non-marital intimate partner violence
- Non-domestic violence

It should be noted that this categorisation is for the purpose of documentation and clarity, and should not obscure the fact that women who approach the Special Cells often experience more than one type of violence in their life. Often, one life problem overlaps with, and triggers, other issues. A woman's attempts to resolve one issue may inspire her to stand up for her rights in more than one sphere, and may inadvertently cause more issues to emerge which constantly require supportive case work. Therefore, all the data listed in the quarterly report under the heading 'Reason for Referral' are multiple responses answers.

Violence With Husband/marital Family as the Perpetrator

Most of the women coming to the Special Cell report domestic violence involving the husband or his family as the perpetrator. In **Figure 12** we show the various kinds of abuse faced by these women. These are not mutually exclusive categories, as the woman usually has to face multiple forms of harassment. It may be noted here that the woman may have undergone either a legally or a socially-sanctioned form of marriage.

A large majority of the cases that come to the Special Cells are cases of physical and mental abuse by the husband (57% and 61% respectively). As many as 38% of women complained of financial harassment by husband. 15% reported sexual abuse from their husband including 16 women who revealed they were forced to undergo an abortion or tubectomy. We surmise that taboos associated with the subject makes it difficult for women to divulge such details. It could also be that few women are aware of their sexual rights – they comply with their husband's wishes until the abuse takes an extreme form.

Figure 12: Violence with husband as the perpetrator

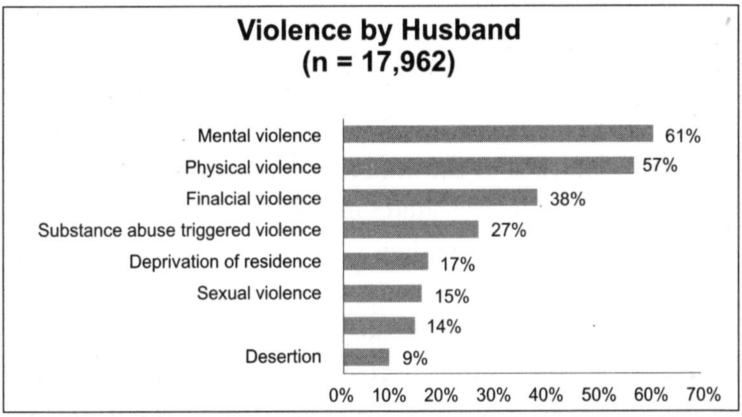

The marital family is also named for physical abuse (29%) and mental abuse (28%). A popular perception especially propagated by the media is that 'a woman's worst enemy is another woman'. In cases of marital violence, the mother-in-law is thought to be the main culprit, while the husband is perceived as a helpless spectator. *Our data show that women have more frequently named the husband as the aggressor than the marital family, which includes the mother-in-law. Earlier studies too have found physical and mental harassment by the husband to be the most frequently reported form of violence.* (Special Cell 1994; Dave & Solanki 2001).

One means of harassment is for a man to disown his marital obligations by throwing his wife out of the marital home, or by leaving the home himself. Our data reveal that 17% of women clients reported being thrown out of the marital home and 9% reported that their husband left the home and deserted them. Another way to view this is that approximately one in five clients at the Special Cells lost their shelter, and another one in ten report being abandoned.

Domestic violence affects more than just the woman – in 5% of cases, members of the wife's natal family have also been made a target of violence by the husband. The data of the Special Cells report that about 6% of cases are ones in which children were the target of violence. This small number does not, of course, cover the indirect psychological and social consequences of being exposed to violence or the indirect effects of possible financial harassment faced by the child's mother – in other words, how parent breakups affect children.

In 2% of cases, the violence was so severe that the woman attempted suicide and a police case followed. In four cases, family members registered a case at the Cell after the woman lost her life.

Four women complained of physical and mental violence from their ex-husband, indicating that dissolution of the marital relationship does not guarantee an end to harassment. Such harassment may also take the form of refusal to give *streedhan* or maintenance (6%), refusal to give custody of children (5%) or refusal of visiting rights to children (2%). In addition, one woman client reported that her husband's first wife perpetrated violence on her, while it was the reverse in four cases – harassment from second wives. (Here, it should be noted that the Special Cells recognise and affirm the right of both women to a violence-free life).

Many other types of marital violence are listed in the six-monthly reports. Even though the number of women who approach the Cell with these problems are small, this indicate the various ways in which a woman can face harassment by her husband and the marital family. These include forcible abortion and tubectomy (16 cases), woman's HIV status leading to harassment (14 cases), mental illness of husband (eight cases), forcible divorce (eight cases) and sexual violence by marital family (four cases). Our data show that more than one fourth of the women (27%) feel harassed because of alcoholism and substance abuse by their husbands. One in five client women faced dowry demands (20%).

Figure 13: Violence with marital family and husband as the perpetrator

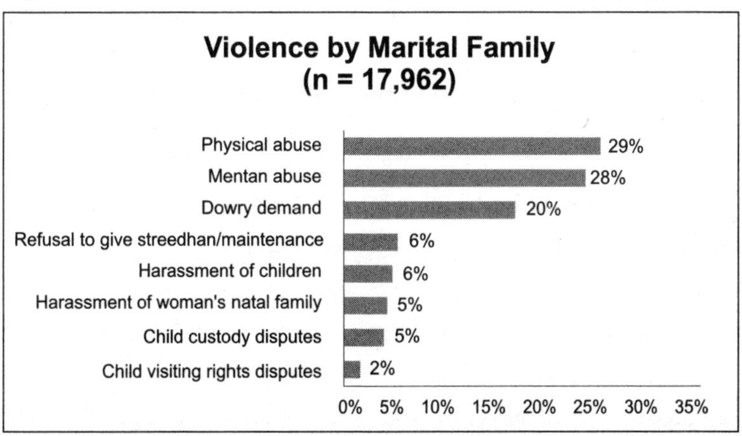

Cases Registered by Husbands

While describing the gender profile of clients, we reported that 12% of cases were registered by men. Even though some of these are cases registered on behalf of women in distress (5%), in other instances husbands have registered complaints against their wives. As stated earlier, such cases are registered at the Cell because they give an entry point to help the woman in the relationship, who, more often than not, is the victim rather than the perpetrator of violence.

Table 5 presents the reasons that married male clients report for requiring the services of the Special Cells. Anecdotal reports of social workers at the Special Cells reveal that the wife is more likely to be the victim than the perpetrator of violence. In 4% of cases of alleged 'desertion by wife', the wife was found to have left home after the violence at home became unbearable.

In 2% of cases of 'harassment by wife', the 'harassing' behaviour of the wife was found to be in retaliation to the violence perpetrated by husband. Occasionally men make complaints of their wife engaging in a relationship outside marriage (19 cases), which in some instances is revealed to be a manifestation of the suspicious nature and the possessiveness of the husband. In some instances, men have complained about interference and harassment from the wife's natal family (46 cases) and of victimisation of the children by the wife (3 cases).

Table 5: Cases registered by husbands

Cases registered by husbands	Number (Percentage)
Desertion by wife	746 (4%)
Harassment by wife	380 (2%)
Harassment by wife's natal family	46 (.3%)
Relationship outside marriage by wife	19 (.1%)
Child battering / Neglect by wife	3 (.02%)

Violence in Non-marital Intimate Partner Relationships

Non-marital intimate partner relationships refer to cohabiting (live-in) as well as non-cohabiting couples who share an intimate relationship without a legally or socially sanctioned form of marriage. This includes same sex partners.

The most frequently registered complaint in this category is 'breach of trust' (5%). That is, women come to the Special Cells when the partner refuses to honour the promise of marriage. We found that such cases of breach of trust have decreased by 90% (from 10% of all cases in 2003 to 0.91% in 2012). This could be because more women are willing to commit to such a relationship without the aim of eventually converting it into a marital relationship, or that more men are entering such relationships without verbal commitments. As many as 56 cases of violence in live-in relationships were registered in the Special Cells over the ten-year period. Two cases reported violence in same-sex relationships. As in case of marital relationships, in six cases the harassment extended even after the termination of the intimate relationship.

Domestic Violence Other than Marital/Non-marital Intimate Partner Violence

Besides the other types of violence reported thus far, our data show that not only intimate partners, other blood relatives may also be perpetrators of violence. About 2% of the clients have approached the Special Cells with complaints of harassment from their natal family members. Some have reported violence that pertained to property disputes in the family (3%). Another 2% of the clients sought help from the Special Cells regarding violence from their son, daughter or daughter-in-law.

In seven cases, children have approached the Cell with the complaint of mental violence from their parents. Child marriage is an age-old form of violence perpetrated on minor girls and in the ten-year assessment period, the Special Cells handled four such cases. The programme's then existing form of reporting does not allow us to examine the age of these child clients.

Non-domestic Violence

Besides violence in the home or within intimate relationships, there are other forms of violence against women. The Special Cells deal with such cases though they are fewer in number. In 2% of the cases registered at the Special Cells, they were of sexual harassment or molestation. This includes many kinds of offenses such as stalking, making obscene comments, groping and obscene exhibition. In 40 cases, the sexually abused person was a minor. In addition, ten cases of trafficking/ forcing sex work and 72 cases of rape were registered at the Special Cells.

Even a decade ago, 44 women registered a complaint of sexual harassment at the workplace, 174 women reported mental harassment at the workplace and 27 reported physical harassment at the workplace. There were also instances of harassment by neighbour/landlord (1.28%).

Cyber-crime has emerged as a new form of sexual harassment involving internet and mobile phones (five cases), and social media. Some examples of cyber-crime are cyber stalking (following a person's movement across the internet), cyber morphing (posting a person's photograph on the internet after obscene editing) and making obscene calls/sending SMSs.

The following case study is an example of the intervention by a Special Cell in such cases:

> Shweta, a middle-class college student from a small town and a conservative family, approached the Special Cell with the

> complaint that she was getting obscene calls on her mobile. The worker persuaded Shweta that she should take the help of the Cyber Crime Branch of the police force, assuring her that confidentiality would be maintained. Within a few hours, the police traced the mobile number from which the calls were being made. They found that the person making the obscene calls was Akshay, who was studying in the same college as Shweta. He had shown an interest in her though she had ignored him. With the help of the police, Akshay was asked to report to the Special Cell. When the social worker confronted Akshay and informed him of the possible consequences of his act, he acknowledged his behaviour, apologised and agreed never to repeat the offence. As Shweta was not keen to pursue further punitive action, he was let off with a warning.

The Special Cells have also been asked to intervene in cases where women have felt themselves to be mistreated by other social groups or organisations: women who have been made a target of violence because of their caste (two cases), negligence by doctor (one case), cheating by financial organisation (one case), cheating/harassment by school authorities (one case). There were eight cases of missing family members and three cases of kidnapping of minor daughter. Such cases are registered in the Special Cell as the Cell workers can support them to get police help to trace the missing person, as well as work with the person and the family after she is found.

Certain categories of cases in the data raise more questions than answers: Cases under the heading 'black magic' (three cases), 'economic offence' (two cases), 'harassment from opposite party' (five cases) and 'sex determination' (two cases).

Figures at a glance:

- 87% of the clients of the Special Cell are women. However, the number of men approaching the Cell has apparently also increased over the ten-year period. Some of them (5%), as fathers and brothers, approach the Special Cell on behalf of the violated woman but there are also cases of men complaining against women (7%). Such cases are accepted at the Cell as a way of approaching the woman in the relationship, who usually is in need of help.
- 72% of clients are women between the age of 18 to 34 years: 42% comprising the sub-group 25 to 34 years. This is where the most visible increase has occurred over the ten-year period.
- Almost a quarter of the women (23%) report functional literacy. It signifies that the service has been able reach to a segment of the population which is likely to have access to fewer resources.
- The most frequently reported problem at the Special Cells is domestic violence involving the husband or his family as the perpetrator with physical and mental abuse by the husband being reported by 57% and 61% of women respectively.
- There were 56 cases of violence in live-in relationship registered at the Special Cells over the ten-year period.

Previous Interventions and Referral Sources

This section focuses on where women clients have sought help previously, as well as on how they heard about the Special Cells. We also contrast the findings from the current analysis against findings from previous analyses of the records from the Special Cells, to understand whether the needs of women have evolved and changed over the years.

Previous Non-Special Cell Interventions

Very few of the women who have come to the Special Cells for help had come without trying other sources of intervention. These sources of previous intervention are shown in **Figure 14**. The data show that 43% of women have first turned to their parents for help. Domestic violence is still perceived as a 'private affair' or a family affair, and a majority of the women seek outside help only after the failure of attempts to resolve the dispute 'within the family'.

Previous interventions also include interventions by acquaintances (2%), prominent members in the community (1%), village panchayat and other government organisations (2%), semi-government organisations such as Tanta Mukta Gaon Sanghatana (TMGS) – a group of villagers authorised to deal with local disputers-56 cases), hospitals and rehabilitation centers (73 cases), religious organisations (20 cases), and educational (4 cases) as well as correctional institutions (22 cases).

In 39% of cases, the police have intervened before referring the case to the Special Cells. Reports from the social workers indicate that many women had approached the Social Service Branch (SSB) of the police force or the Mahila Takrar Nivaran Kaksha (MTNK). Some had approached police stations. In such instances, the police might have registered a non-cognisable complaint, they might have temporarily detained the perpetrator under Section 110 of the Mumbai Police Act, or they may have attempted mediation of the dispute. Often these interventions fail to prevent recurrence of the violence. 6% of women have approached other NGOs prior to coming to the Cell. 5% of clients have attempted to find a legal solution to their problem through the court and 2% through lawyers. In 1.8% of cases, women reported approaching the caste panchayat for mediation.

Figure 14: Previous interventions

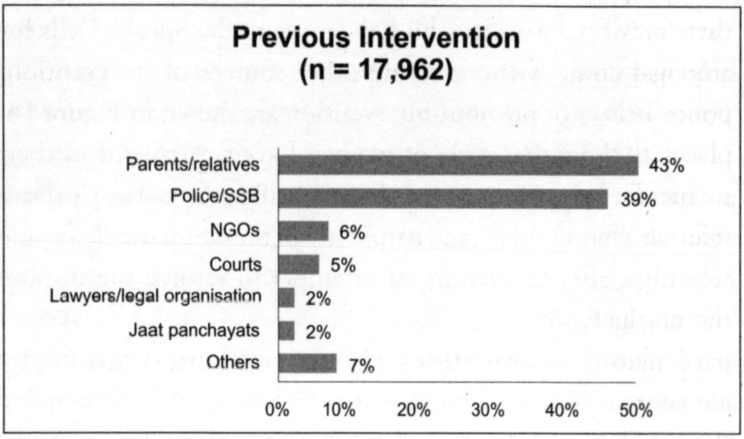

Sources of client referral

Figure 15 shows that more than one-third of the referrals to the Special Cells are from ex-clients (37%). Such a high number of referrals from ex-clients suggest that women receiving services from the Special Cells are satisfied with the help received at the Cells. Such referrals from women who have earlier benefited from the services of the Special Cells may be direct – such as informing another woman facing violence about the Special Cells or accompanying the woman to the Cell. Referrals from ex-clients may also be indirect – for instance, word-of-mouth information of other women benefiting reaches the violated woman (8%) or her family/acquaintances/ employers (9%).

Referrals from the police form one-fourth of the total referrals (26%). This includes referrals from SSB and MTNK. Such referrals reflect the continued confidence that the Special Cells have been able to generate within the system regarding their ability to help the survivors of domestic violence. In stark contrast, referrals through police helplines are extremely few (0.7%). This could be due to a number of reasons: Helplines are a newer phenomenon for the period of data collection, and there may not have been enough awareness about these services amongst the general population at the time. In some places the police helpline was not fully functional at that time. In a few places, the helplines are operated by MTNK, which may choose to handle the calls using its own resources without further referral. The low volume of referrals from police helplines as recently as 2012 indicates that there is still room for improving the engagement of the Special Cells with the police system; particularly, to ensure that all police personnel in the district are aware of the availability of a woman-centric service within their own structure.

About 10% of referrals are from NGOs including organisations working for women, 5% from local social workers and 5% are from lawyers and legal organisations. Other sources of referrals include government organisations, semi-government organisations such as Tanta Mukta Gaon Sanghatana, *Jaat panchayats* and religious organisations. Traditional social groups such as caste panchayats (170 cases) and religious organisations (16 cases) have also sent cases to the Special Cells. It is interesting to note that caste panchayats are active in a district such as Dhule (5.9%), as well as in a cosmopolitan area of a metro city such as the Comissioner's office (4.19%).

The percentage of clients being referred by government organisations such as ICDS (93 cases), village panchayats (79 cases) and semi-government organisations such as TMGS (13 cases) is negligible, indicating a greater need for more networking/awareness programmes with them. Referrals from medical and paramedical organisations are low (1%). This could either be because hospitals prefer to deal with the cases of VAW themselves, or because they may lack the expertise to detect cases.

Some women approached the Special Cells after obtaining information about the scheme from the media (1%). In the latter part of the ten-year period, some women in Mumbai reported that they came to know about the Special Cells through the internet (eight cases). The Special Cells are featured as a service for violated women on Just Dial (a local search engine providing contact information for various services), but *the programme does not have its own website, nor does it find a mention in the police website. Some more thought may be given to using the internet to make this service accessible to a wider population.*

The number of women referred by the court to the Special Cells are very few (154). In addition, some referrals come through the Protection of Women from Domestic Violence Act, 2005 (PWDVA). After 2009, clients have been referred to Special Cells' social workers working as Protection Officers (33) because in that year as per the order of the Government of Maharashtra, some of the Special Cells' personnel were designated to perform the duties of Protection Officers under the PWDVA. However, the directions of the government in this respect were not clear, so the number of referrals is not high. Other protection workers appointed by the government have also referred cases to the Special Cells (36%), because the Special Cells personnel have been designated as service providers under the Act by the Maharashtra government.

We also sought to understand changes across the ten-year period in the pattern of referrals. To do this we plotted running averages of the data for the last ten years for referrals from ex-clients, the police and NGOs (Figure 16). The graph clearly demonstrates that over the ten-year period, referrals from the police and ex-clients have been rising while referrals from the NGOs appear to have remained steady.

Figure 15: Sources of client referral

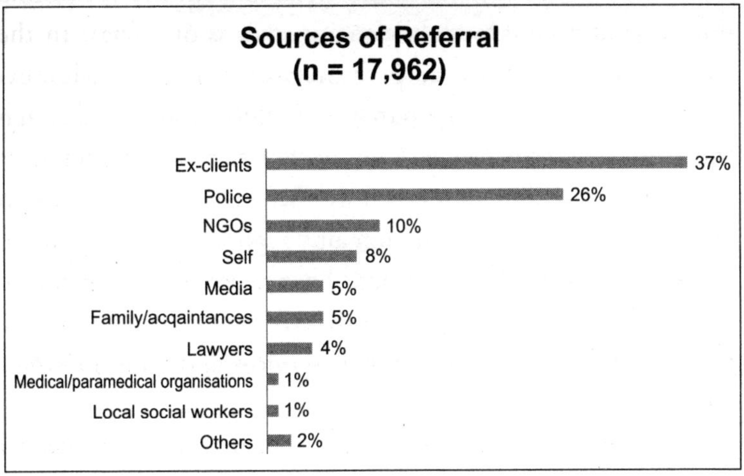

To further our understanding of the referrals to Special Cells, we contrasted the pattern of referrals in the current review with those reported in the earlier studies: namely Special Cell for Women and Children (1994), Dave and Solanki (2001) and Apte (2004), represented in **Figure** 17.

Figure 16: Sources of client referral: Year-wise trends

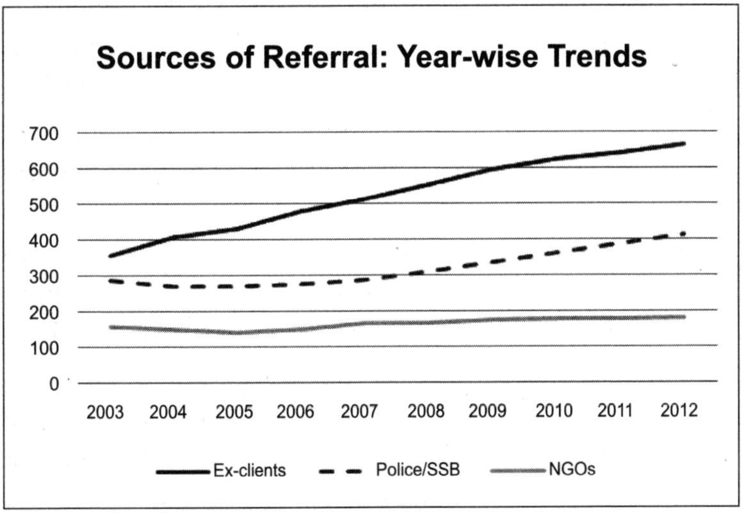

Our first observation was that in all four studies, the police, ex-clients and NGOs are the major sources of referral to the Cells. In the 1994 study, the percentage of clients referred by ex-clients was 6%. This shot up to 41% in 2001, clearly indicating the trust that the Special Cells have been able to generate regarding the quality of services. In the current ten-year period the referrals from ex-clients remains high at 38% despite the number of new Cells established. That referrals from ex-clients continue to be very high reflects that the Special Cells continue to maintain a reputation for their services and a high level of client satisfaction.

With regard to police referrals, the percentage of clients referred is higher in the studies done in 2004 (28%), and in the current study (26%) as compared to the earlier two studies undertaken in 1994 (16%) and 2001 (13%). One explanation could be that new Cells were established in rural Maharashtra after 2001, at the SP offices of Aurangabad, Nasik, Nanded, Yavatmal, Wardha, Dhule and Pune districts. The high numbers may reflect increased awareness about, and acceptance of, the services of the Special Cells in the police system due to extensive groundwork with them during the process of making the Cells functional. Further, in the rural areas, there could be a paucity of other NGOs providing services to violated women and the Special Cells may be the only avenue for help for survivors of violence.

The percentage of clients referred by NGOs in the present study is visibly less than that found in the studies done in 1994, 2001 and 2004. With the expansion of the Special Cells project, there was an increase in the number of clients approaching the Special Cells. The outreach activities undertaken by these Cells also contributed to an increase in the awareness in the general population and among the police about the services provided by the Special Cells. Because of this, it is possible that more and more people started coming to the Cells through ex-clients and the police, and did not need to go to other NGOs to get information about the Special Cells.

Figure 17: Comparison of referral sources with earlier studies

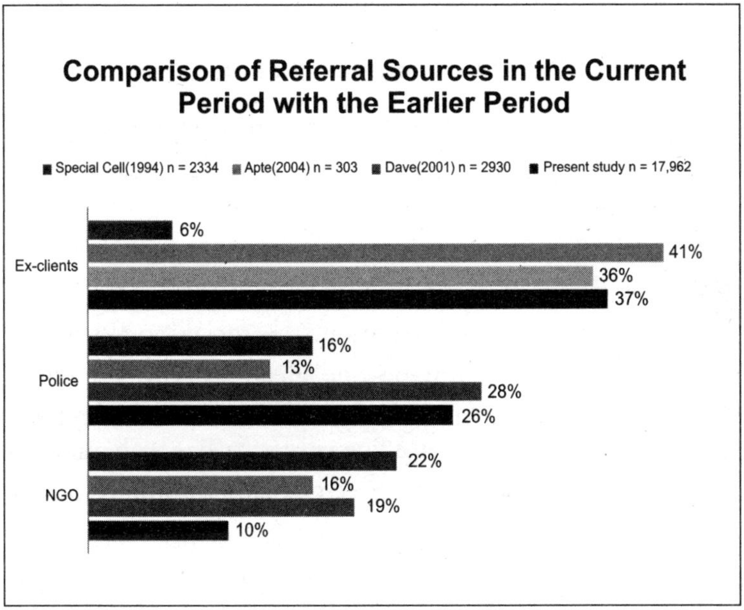

Figures at a glance:

- Most women approach the Special Cells for assistance after trying other avenues.
- 43% of women first sought help from their natal family.
- 39% of women first sought help from the police.
- Referrals from ex-clients continue to be very high over the years, indicating that the Special Cells continue to maintain a reputation for their services and a high level of client-satisfaction. Police referrals account for one-fourth of all clients (26%).

Interventions Work of the Special Cell

While previous sections covered details of the client volume in general, and then explored the client profile more specifically, this section focuses on reports of the different types of activities that the social workers based at the Special Cells undertake. These are summarised from their monthly reports. These reports have been compiled from 2006 onwards.

Interventions Undertaken on Behalf of the Client

To assist the survivors of violence who register at the Special Cells, social workers engage in the following intervention strategies and process:

Individual Meetings

During the course of intervention, the social worker at the Special Cell conducts one-on-one meetings with the client to give support, information, guidance. She/he conducts individual meetings with the perpetrator of the abuse as well, to understand their perceptions, and to work towards changing attitudes and behaviour patterns causing violence. She/he also conducts individual meetings with significant others to build or rebuild a support network for the woman survivor of violence. **Table 6** shows that the number of individual meetings has nearly doubled over the course of seven years (2006 to 2012).

Joint Meetings

These are meetings in which two or more individuals with opposing viewpoints, usually the client and the perpetrator of violence, are brought together at the Cell. Through discussions and negotiations, the social worker helps them to arrive at mutually agreeable arrangements aimed at ensuring a violence-free life for the woman. The worker performs the role of a facilitator at these meetings. The number of joint meetings has also doubled in the period from 2006 to 2012. (Table 6).

Home Visits and Collateral Visits

A visit to the house where the woman is residing or the house of significant others in the case is an important tool for the social workers for many reasons. Home visits help to strengthen the relationship of the worker and the client, assess the crisis that the client is going through, establish contact with significant actors in the environment, as well as maintain follow-ups of the client after the intervention. Collateral visits are made to police stations, shelter homes, hospitals and panchayat groups for the purpose of building support networks for the woman. Matching the increase in cases coming into the Special Cells, home visits and collateral visits also show an increase (Table 6).

Table 6: Client-related interventions summarised from the monthly reports

	2006	2007	2008	2009	2010	2011	2012
Individual meetings	5,758	6,403	5,533	6,328	6,999	7,719	10,202
Joint meetings	2,110	2,505	2,414	2338	2,669	2,679	4,218
Home visits & collateral visits	1,639	1,389	1,426	1478	1,605	1,693	2,234
Cases where police help was sought	502	457	5,22	575	630	628	650

Cases in Which Police Help was Sought

Social workers at the Special Cells may work with the police to reach the perpetrator of violence, to get child custody or to recover streedhan. As seen in Table 6, the number of cases where police help has been sought has been more or less consistent throughout the years from 2006 to 2012.

Work Under the PWDVA

The Protection of Women from Domestic Violence Act, 2005 is a comprehensive legislation aimed at tackling domestic violence. The Special Cells' personnel are designated as Service Providers under the Act. The monthly reports consulted for this particular assessment provide data for five years – from 2008 to 2012, regarding the work of the Cells under the Act.

There is a noticeable increase in the number of clients referred by the social workers at the Special Cells to the court or to Protection Officers (PO) under this Act, which has almost doubled (Table 7).

The number of clients being referred to the Cells under this capacity appears to have increased four-fold. However, in comparison to the number of women approaching the Special Cell for help, the number of women opting to seek help under PWDV Act is much smaller. This indicates that to deal with the violence in their lives, women expect and receive many other types of interventions from the Special Cell and not just referral under the PWDV Act.

The monthly reports capture the reported activities of social workers at the Special Cells who were designated as Protection Officers by the State government after 2005. However, as the government directions in this respect were not clear, and as other protection officers were subsequently appointed by the government, some social workers stopped undertaking the responsibilities of a Protection Officer (though they continue to respond actively to reported cases of domestic violence). For this reason, the number of clients registered by the social workers under the category of themselves as PO shows an initial increase and then a decline (**Table** 7).

Thus, the Protection of Women from Domestic Violence Act is increasingly utilised by the Special Cells' social workers to seek redressal for the grievances of violated women, even though there is need for clarity on their role as Protection Officers.

Table 7: PWDVA-related interventions summarised from the Monthly Reports

	2008	2009	2010	2011	2012
Clients referred by Special Cells to Protection Officer/the court under PWDVA	183	180	185	206	306
Clients referred to Special Cells under PWDVA	23	33	75	102	101
Clients registered by the Special Cells' workers as Protection Officers	-	-	48	89	29

Work at the Macro Level

Besides working with individual clients or their families, the social workers at the Special Cells also address issues of VAW at the macro level through awareness-building activities, advocacy for law and policy change and dissemination of information related to the issue of violence against women on various forums. This work is presented in **Table 8**.

Though it still forms a sizeable chunk of the work done by the social workers at the Special Cells, the participation of the social workers in the programme/seminars/workshops seems to have diminished across the seven-year period. This could be due to the increase in caseload. At the same time, it should be noted that the Cell workers are being increasingly called upon to act as resource persons at various workshops, indicating an increasing acknowledgement of their knowledge and expertise in the field of violence against women as well as perhaps a growing awareness in the community of their skills.

Table 8: Macro-level work of the Special Cells

	2006	2007	2008	2009	2010	2011	2012
Special Cell invited as resource person for workshop	-	-	3	55	185	184	137
Programmes organised by the Special Cell	130	105	85	132	44	37	96
Participation in workshops	466	392	383	349	213	268	298

Thus, we see that from 2006 to 2012, the number of individual meetings, joint meetings, home visits and collateral visits has steadily increased – in keeping with the increase in the number of clients. The number of cases in which police help was sought, however, has been largely consistent between 2006-2012. As per Table 7, there is a noticeable increase in the number of clients referred by the Cell workers to the court or to Protection Officers under PWDV Act, though the number is far less than the number of women seeking help from the Special Cells.

From the data available, we can effectively conclude that there is a need for the kind of services the Special Cell offers, evidenced by the growing number of clients, and the rapid increase in referrals from ex-clients as compared to previous decades. Data on ex-client referrals reflects a growing awareness about these services, as well as an endorsement of their value.

The police remains an important source of referral for the Cells, as well as a source of intervention support. Women from the reproductive age group continue to be the primary clients at the Special Cells, with the age demographics remaining largely similar to previous decades; and women continue to face interlinked and diverse forms of violence in their lives. A majority of clients faced violence from their husbands and marital families before approaching the Special Cells, and had tried other means of intervention including families, police, and the community.

The learning has been, women are often reluctant to approach institutions in the first instance, and seek support from social networks before resorting to institutional support. Another trend observed was the increasing number of male clients – either approaching the Cell on behalf of a woman (usually a family member), or complaining against a woman. The Special Cell's policy on such cases is to engage with these men as an opportunity to approach a woman who may be facing violence and remain committed to feminist social work intervention principles through this engagement.

Data on the interventions work at the Special Cell reveals that direct interventions work through individual and joint meetings has increased significantly over the seven-year period studied. An important development for this period was the introduction of the PWDV Act and an increase in referrals under the Act, due to the social workers' roles as Protection Officers appointed under the Act. The interventions work of the Cells, thus, continues to keep pace with the growing volume of clients, and adapt and grow as new mechanisms of redressal emerge. The next chapter explores the interventions work of the Cells in greater depth, through case studies, to illustrate how casework across this decade continues to uphold the guiding principles of the Special Cell's intervention practice.

A Review of Case Records from the Special Cells

IN THE PREVIOUS chapter, we drew from quantitative monitoring data in order to understand who accesses the Cell, and assessed the growth in clientele and work over the decade following expansion in Maharashtra. The previous chapter described the work of the Special Cells in numbers derived from the monthly and quarterly reports.This section puts names and faces to the numbers. It attempts to describe the complex nature of the social work intervention at the Cells through case stories – highlighting women's diverse experiences, and the adaptations and solutions social workers must find while remaining committed to feminist social work praxis. We used case records from the Cells to illustrate the multi-pronged nature of the social work intervention practiced. Some of these case records have been collated from the quarterly reports of the various Special Cells, some have been related to the authors by social workers, and some have been observed and documented by the authors themselves at the Special Cells. Names of clients have been changed to protect their identity.

Feminist Social Work Intervention Practices

This chapter is organised on the basis of the interventions described in the ten monitoring indicators of the Special Cells. The monitoring indicators were developed in 2002 by the Strategic Management Group comprising Social Workers, the Special Cell coordinators, and the TISS faculty-in-charge over the course of extensive consultation with social workers of the Special Cells, and emerged organically from the work and practice of the Cell. The Cell holds several principles as non-negotiable components of its work: women's right to self-determination and a violence-free life, a pro-woman, feminist social work perspective, an emphasis on systemic as well as individual engagement, and an emphasis on building a strategic partnership with the police in order to address violence against women and promote systemic accountability and change.

The monitoring indicators of the Cell are integral guiding principles of the work and have remained relevant to the interventions practice even to the present day. This chapter, thus, analyses case records using the monitoring indicators as analytical categories, in order to present a holistic picture of the kind of work done by the Special Cells. The feminist principles and scope of work relating to each monitoring indicator have been detailed, followed by case studies relating to this theme. The chapter is therefore divided into the following themes, each corresponding to a different monitoring indicator:

- Strengthening the psychological self of the violated woman
- Working with the perpetrators and significant others in the life of the violated woman

- Building support systems for the violated woman
- Engaging the police for helping the violated woman
- Facilitating the violated women's journey through the criminal justice system
- Arranging shelter for violated women
- Working with men in the interest of the violated women
- Re-establishment of violated women's rights over their economic assets
- Rehabilitation counselling

Providing Emotional Support and Strengthening the Psychological Self of the Violated Woman

All women coming to the Special Cells for help require emotional support, regardless of the issue that brought them to the Cell. They also require facilitative assistance in restoring their lost confidence and rebuilding their sense of self-worth. Social workers at the Special Cells are trained to do this by embodying social work principles and values.

Active Participation and Self-determination

One key social work value is the client's right to self-determination. Social workers focus on enabling a woman realise her agency and autonomy and then enabling her to exercise it. For instance, during a casework session in the Special Cell, if students or personnel from the support team are visiting the Cell for observation, the client is first asked if she will grant permission for them to be present during the session, and her decision must be adhered to.

A woman survivor approaching the Cell may expect 'advice' or 'directions'. However, at the Special Cell, rather than providing a ready-made solution, the woman is helped to get a clearer understanding of her problem, make a realistic assessment of her situation, explore all the available options, and arrive at a decision regarding the future course of action herself. Special Cell workers respect women survivors as experts on their own individual situations and respect the decision of the client. This is sometimes difficult to practice in cases of domestic violence, where the social worker faces tension between concern for the client's safety and respecting the client's right to assess the danger of her situation.

In some instances, when working with violated women, Cell workers come across situations where a woman makes a choice to return to an abusive husband/partner, or initiates contact with a partner against whom she has filed a criminal case or makes other choices that may compromise her safety or that of her children. In these instances, the social worker may speak about these concerns to the woman, but in a non-judgmental way, that always leaves room for the client to disagree and chose her own course of action. The social worker helps the client to create a safety plan in such cases, while respecting the client's decision.

The social worker attempts to restore self-confidence by building the problem-solving abilities of the client. She/he shows faith in the woman and helps her to participate actively in her own case by encouraging her to perform tasks on her own, such as writing the initial application, coming to the Cell unescorted, approaching a police station and other agencies independently, gathering details and documentary evidence, etc. She also encourages the woman to take responsibility for keeping appointments and following up at the Cell, and to make her own decisions after actively analysing her situation and exploring possible options. She is also encouraged to voice her own needs during meetings with other stakeholders such as the police.

Non-judgmental Attitude and Strengths-based Approach

The Special Cell social workers emphasise acceptance of the woman as a person, being non-judgmental, and validating the woman's experience of violence. For instance, the client may, in the course of sharing her situation, reveal that she has had an out-of-marriage relationship. The social worker attempts to demonstrate warmth and acceptance irrespective of her personal values or beliefs. She also listens carefully and gives legitimacy to her concerns and fears. The social worker at the Special Cell also contributes to the restoration of the survivor's psychological self by reminding her of her abilities and of her past achievements. The survivor is enabled to see the support system within which she may attempt to rebuild her life.

Critical Social Perspective

The social worker encourages women survivors to see themselves as persons first, and then as persons within relationships with roles and responsibilities. A woman in India is socialised to think of herself as a daughter, a mother, a sister and a wife rather than as a person in her own right, and to subsume her own wishes, desires and goals in favour of these socially prescribed roles. Part of strengthening the woman is to assist her to challenge these patriarchal attitudes and stereotyped gender roles.

Finally, the Special Cell worker helps the woman client to see her problem in a larger social context and with a broader perspective; not just as triggered by specific precipitating factors, but as a manifestation of the unequal relationship between men and women in a largely patriarchal society. The social worker makes her aware that the roots of her problems lie in the larger societal myths and expectations pertaining to gender roles. The worker helps her to understand that removing that trigger factor will not translate into the end of violence unless she is strong enough to challenge her subjugation. For example, a woman who attributes her battering by her husband to his drinking habits is helped to see that it is usually the wife who gets beaten by the alcoholic man and not, for instance, his employer.

The social worker in countering patriarchal conditioning may also serve as a role model to women, as the confidence and competence demonstrated by the female workers often inspires confidence in the woman approaching the Cell for help.

The following case illustrations highlight some of these various steps through the stories of three clients of the Special Cells:

Case 1

Case details: Anita, a 23-year-old commerce graduate from a middle class background had tried to commit suicide because of marital violence and lack of support from her father.

Intervention: The social worker, after active listening, helped her to realise the she was well educated, that she still had the support from her extended family and that she could take up a job and use the facility of a working women's hostel. This enabled Anita to gather her courage to consider other ways of getting out of her violent home. In this case, the social worker helped her rebuild her psychological self by reminding her of her past achievements.

Case 2

Case details: Neerja had an inter-religious marriage, which her family had bitterly opposed. The husband began abusing Neerja physically after some time, and she had to leave her marital home. Neerja's natal family remained unsupportive. Neerja had studied up till the 12th standard, had weak eyesight, and was physically very weak.

Intervention: Neerja was able to stay in her natal home because of intervention from the Special Cell. She had a six-month old son who was at that point in the custody of her husband. Because of her physical disability and economic dependence, Neerja was apprehensive about her ability to care for her child economically or otherwise. The husband wanted Neerja to have custody of the child. The natal family as well as social acquaintances expressed shock that Neerja was not keen to fight for the custody of the child. It took a lot of reassurance and support from the social worker for Neerja to stick to her decision of giving the custody of the child to the father. Thus, the social worker had helped Neerja to acknowledge her own needs and make a decision based on her own understanding of the realities in her life, demonstrated non-judgmental acceptance when Neerja voiced a wish to go against the customary practice of society, and helped her to work past the role expectations placed on her with regard to being a 'proper mother'.

Case 3

Case details: Gita came to the Cell because of mental harassment from her in-laws and sexual violence from her husband (related to the issue of dowry and the fact that she had delivered a female child). She had lost her appetite, suffered from insomnia, and had contemplated suicide. She was caught between going back to her violent husband and depriving her daughter of a father.

Intervention: The Special Cell social worker counselled her, bringing her to the realisation that her life was important and worth living. She helped her to stop blaming herself for the failure of her marriage. Throughout this process, the Cell worker showed patience and moved at the client's pace. The Cell worker put effort into building her confidence and self-esteem. Since Gita was keen to study further, the Cell worker encouraged her to explore the internet for future courses. Gita resumed her education and took up a job. She was also given sexual counselling. The worker told her to read books on the subject to lessen her feelings of sexual inadequacy. The Cell worker undertook many efforts to help Gita think about herself rather than focusing on others. Gita needed a lot of time and support to accept that it was not a crime to think of her own happiness. She realised that she could make other people happy only when she became emotionally stable herself. The social worker also attempted to show her that small children needed holistic love, affection and a secure environment rather than a 'family' in the conventional sense of the word. After many discussions regarding her options, Gita decided to seek a divorce. In this case, the social worker proceeded inch by inch, at the pace of the client. She set in place one by one the bricks needed to rebuild the shattered façade of Gita's self-confidence. Decision-making took place when the client was ready.

Negotiating for Non-violence with Various Stakeholders

This section describes negotiations to stop violence with the perpetrators and significant others in the life of the violated women. The term 'significant others' takes on a wider meaning at the Special Cells. Often these are the persons who are either inflicting violence on the woman or who, through inaction and silence, condone it. These are the stakeholders with whom the social workers of the Cells work with the intention of brokering an agreement of non-violence. Sometimes significant others have to be urged to protect the woman survivor. The social worker aims to imprint firmly and indelibly on the minds of these stakeholders that violence is non-negotiable, that its effects are damaging and that every human being has an innate right to protection from violence.

The worker prepares the client for these negotiations by helping her to be aware of her rights and by expanding her own understanding of why violence occurs. Then, the social worker will attempt to devise strategies to stop the violence. During joint meetings with perpetrators of violence, the worker strives to create an environment where the woman can speak for herself without being dominated or feeling inhibited. The social worker takes special care not to antagonise the perpetrators, rather he/she strives to make them understand the client's needs and rights and to recognise the benefits they get by respecting the client's decisions. She allows the perpetrators time to adjust and reconcile with this new perspective. Her goal is to enlist them as her allies in the negotiation for change. The lengthy and delicate process of negotiating with the stakeholders is illustrated through these cases:

Case 1

Case details: Jasmin was being physically and mentally abused by her husband. Finally, when she decided to raise her voice against the abuse and approach police and other organisations, he began to abuse her sexually, with the justification that her body was his possession.

Intervention: The social worker stressed in the meeting with the husband that the woman had the basic right to live a life of her choice and that force or pressure violated these human rights. Jasmin also needed assurance that this situation was not her fault. Over the course of multiple meetings, the Cell worker prepared her to feel capable of speaking to her husband about the sexual violence in the joint meetings at the Cell. Here we see that the social worker had to work with both the client and her partner in order to handle this delicate conversation.

Case 2

Case details: Neha faced physical and mental harassment by her husband. During her pregnancy in the first year of marriage, she was forced to leave her marital home as she was unable to fulfill their demand for money from her parents. The marital family kept no contact with her during her pregnancy or child birth. But when her son was two years old, they started asking Neha to return with the child. Neha was not prepared to return to her husband. She approached the Special Cell.

Intervention: At the first joint meeting, Haresh was not ready to grant a divorce. Thus, he was permitted time to absorb the fact that Neha's decision was final and that he had to accept it. At the second joint meeting, Haresh continued demanding reconciliation while Neha wanted divorce. The social worker explained to him and to his parents that reconciliation was not possible without Neha's consent, and Neha was not willing to reconcile. She pointed out that if they were not ready for a mutual consent divorce (which was less expensive), then Neha would have to register a case in court which would certainly be more expensive and time-consuming for both parties. The social worker enlisted Haresh's father to convince his son about these points. In the third joint meeting, both Haresh and Neha agreed to a divorce by mutual consent. Neha negotiated for her streedhan and maintenance for her child. Haresh asked for time, but the list of streedhan items was prepared. In the fourth joint meeting the list of streedhan items was mutually finalised. Haresh also agreed to pay maintenance in a lump sum and to give custody of the child to Neha. He cemented his agreement in writing through an assurance paper. Since marriage counselling for mutual consent divorce cases is mandatory in the family court, the social worker contacted a marriage counsellor at the family court, briefed her about the case, and referred Neha and Haresh to her with an appointment. After finalising the decision arrived at the Special Cell, Haresh agreed to provide the agreed-on maintenance through the court. Neha kept the social worker informed about the progress in the court. After six months she obtained the divorce, maintenance, streedhan and child custody. Building relationships with stakeholders to ensure non-violence is a slow process, and the social worker in this case went step by step. She worked with the stakeholders individually, and used the progress in convincing one to change the attitudes of the other members. She also followed up the process at the family court to ensure that this delicate decision would not be shaken.

Building Support Systems for Violated Women

The Special Cells regularly undertake the task of consciousness-raising regarding VAW and women's rights with police personnel, members of the criminal justice system (judges, prosecutors, lawyers and probation officers), members of the health system and other professionals. Attempts are also made to ensure that woman clients are able to access such systems. Social workers also try to build recognition and support for the issues among various social groups such as community-based organisations, educational institutions, and citizen groups. They work to enlist the families of violated women and concerned others as allies in her struggle against her abusive situation. The following illustrations highlight instances of working with a formal system and an informal system respectively:

Case 1

Case details: Ganga, newly married after graduating from high school, was facing severe physical abuse form her alcoholic husband.

Intervention: The medical practitioner of a government facility, where Ganga had gone for medical help after being badly beaten by her husband, refused to specify in his medical certificate the cause of injuries sustained by her. The social worker had to painstakingly explain to him the legal significance of his omission before he rectified the medical certificate to state that the injuries were caused by domestic violence.

Case 2

Case details: Beena was from the Banjara community and had approached her caste panchayat for a divorce because her brother-in-law had attempted to rape her and her husband refused to believe her version or do anything about the attempted rape. As per the panchayat rules, Beena had to pay compensation to her non-supportive husband supposedly in lieu of marriage expenses he had incurred in the past. Beena then obtained her divorce but was unsuccessful in getting her streedhan returned. At this point she approached the Special Cell.

Intervention: The social workers had several meetings with the members of the panchayat. It took a lot of strategising on part of the workers to get the panchayat members to gradually acknowledge the unfairness of the situation, without antagonising them or their rules. In one joint meeting held at the Cell about 40 members of the Banjara Panchayat came to the Cell. After much negotiation, the husband agreed to return Beena's streedhan as well as the unfair compensation amount.

Engaging Police Help in the Interest of Violated Women

Special Cells for Women and Children are strategically located within police stations. This facilitates the use of police help by social workers to assist women survivors of violence.

One strategy for engaging police help is through providing letters to clients that are addressed to their specific local police station. As the stationery on which the letter is written carries the name and address of the Cell (and the corresponding police station), it most likely produces a faster response from the police. Social workers may also accompany clients to the police station (that is, they make a collateral visit) and may have dialogue with police personnel at different levels in the system.

After registering a new client's case and hearing the case history, social workers send out Call Letters to perpetrators identified by the client, requesting them to visit the Cell for an individual or joint meeting. In the event that perpetrators of violence do not respond to these Call Letters or to their telephone calls, social workers may send a message through the wireless network to the concerned police station. The concerned police station will then request the perpetrator to report to the Cell on their behalf – and a request coming directly from the local police station inevitably ensures prompt compliance by the perpetrator.

Police assistance is routinely sought to regain child/infant custody as well as to retrieve the belongings of the woman survivor if she has been thrown out of the marital home. Social workers also use police assistance to challenge the perpetrators of violence, by driving home the point that violence is a crime, so as to deter them from engaging in more violence. Social workers at the Special Cells facilitate efforts by police personnel to find suitable procedural and legal ways to serve the interest of the violated woman, such as registration of criminal cases. The Special Cells also use various means such as training, dialogue and disseminating research findings to assist police personnel in recognising violence against women as a crime, and act as consultants or experts, from whom the police can seek advice on such cases.

The following examples illustrate some of these issues:

Case 1

Case details: Malika had left her marital home after an incident of severe physical abuse. Later she came to the Special Cell and sought the return of her belongings. However, her husband refused to return them.

Intervention: The Special Cell worker approached the police station in whose jurisdiction the marital home fell and explained the situation to the police there. Following this, a police constable accompanied Malika to her marital home to retrieve her belongings. Malika's husband and marital family did not dare to openly express their hostility in the presence of the police personnel and the woman was successful in recovering her possessions.

Case 2

Case details: Sudha, a 23-year-old woman, working as domestic help, approached the Special Cell after her husband poured kerosene on her body.

Intervention: The social worker urged her to file a complaint at the police station. When Sudha went to the police station, she was advised there to register a non-cognisable offence (NC). Doing this would label the incident as less serious, and no preventive action would take place. So the social worker accompanied Sudha to the same police station where she convinced them that preventive action against the man was necessary as there was a real possibility that he could burn Sudha alive in future. The outcome was that the police registered a criminal case against the man.

Case 3

Case details: A local social worker brought Manju, a 13-year-old girl, to the Special Cell who was caught after having run away from home. Manju's family thought that she was having an affair with someone, and had badly thrashed her when she was brought back. Manju said that she had run away as she was scared of her father's anger. Since everybody thought her to be lying, she was brought to the Special Cell.

Intervention: It took some time for the social workers to gain Manju's confidence, who initially told different versions of her story to different people. She finally revealed to the workers that she had been sexually abused by her neighbour for the past three years. Manju's parents were labourers, and used to ask the neighbour to keep an eye on her when they went to work. The neighbour had threatened Manju, telling her that he would kill her parents if she complained to anyone. After abusing her for two years, he bragged about it to other men in the community. Those men also started to blackmail Manju and forced her to have sexual relations with them. Then some boys from her school came to know about this, and they in turn started demanding sexual favours from her. They had forced her to go out with them, when the family thought that she had run away with someone.

When the social worker approached police, the police were not ready to believe the girl's story. They expressed doubts about the girl's character. After a lot of discussion and persuasion, one police officer finally met the girl. He became convinced of the sexual harassment faced by the girl, immediately registered the crime, and took six of the suspects into custody. The girl was sent for medical checkup. At the time of documentation of the case study, the criminal case was still in progress.

Legal Aid to Facilitate the Violated Woman's Journey Through the CJS

Special Cells' social workers help a woman facing abuse to effectively navigate the criminal justice system by providing her with information regarding her legal options under civil, criminal and customary laws. They prepare her for the procedures of the legal system and help her understand the resources required to obtain her rights through the legal route.

They assist her to procure necessary documentation, plan legal strategies, refer clients who need legal aid to lawyers or legal organisations with a pro-woman perspective, and also help clients to register a criminal case where required, to give police statements and to depose as a witness (particularly in cases of sexual offences). Social workers sometimes have to help clients to secure their legal rights such as police protection, and may be required to mobilise other individuals and systems to support the client in her legal battle.

The first case shows how the social worker helped the client by explaining standard court procedures. In the second case, we see how the social worker assists the client in the legal process itself.

Case 1

Case details: Tina was a 20-year-old woman who entered into an arranged marriage. After the wedding, the husband habitually avoided sexual relations with her. Then Tina spotted him in an intimate position with his brother's wife.

Intervention: Tina approached the Special Cell. Here she firmly stated her decision to separate from her husband. The husband was called to the Special Cell where he denied having any sexual relations outside marriage. But he agreed to a mutual consent divorce. The social worker advised the couple that the best time to approach the family court was after completion of the mandatory one year of separation. She explained the court procedures in detail as well as the documents required. She also advised them to reduce unnecessary and exorbitant fees by avoiding civil lawyers.

Case 2

Case Details: The client, Lalita, began to earn her livelihood through tailoring after she was abandoned by her husband. She also began organising the village women for religious activities and Self-Help Groups (Bachat Gat). At this point, Gaja, a villager with a criminal record, started harassing her. Lalita approached the Special Cell, which, with help from the local police, succeeded in stopping the harassment. The anti-social elements in the village, however, continued to be unhappy with Lalita's efforts to organise the village women. During a meeting of the self-help group, somebody deliberately switched off the electricity. A fight broke out between two factions in the village during which Gaja's son was killed. Lalita was arrested and sent to jail on the charge of abetment to murder.

Intervention: The social workers at the Special Cell mobilised lawyers to arrange for her bail. After her release on bail, they helped her to apply for police protection. As there was staff turnover at the police station, the social worker met the new police personnel and oriented them as to the gravity of the situation. She also helped the police to collect evidence. In order to prove that Lalita had been wrongly implicated in the murder case, she requested details of past police complaints registered against Gaja. When the police were evasive in providing these details, she went to higher authorities and with their assistance obtained the release of these details, which became part of the court case. The investigation showed that when the electricity was switched off during the meeting, Lalita had gone to register a complaint at the police station with other women, and so she was not present at the moment of the crime. The women who were potential witnesses were scared to report this, as they had been threatened by Gaja. The Special Cell worker and the police reassured them and persuaded them to give evidence. Their evidence was instrumental in getting Lalita released from jail.

Arranging Shelter for Violated Women

Sometimes a woman client is in crisis because she has lost her shelter. At other times, she may seek assistance for alternate shelter if she feels unable to cope with the violence in her home. The social workers at the Special Cells are trained to provide assistance in such situations. They provide referrals to the woman and/or child for temporary shelter/residence, health services, educational services or financial aid. As a part of making such referrals, they give the client a reality orientation about the facilities available, as well as their limitations, such as rules she may have to follow at a shelter, and may ask her to visit the shelter home before the referral is made.

During her stay in the shelter home the woman may continue to seek help of the Special Cell for any problems. Sometimes the shelter home authorities also approach the Cell if they feel that the woman is experiencing any problem (eg. if the violent husband comes and starts threatening the woman) or if the woman is having trouble adjusting to the rules of the shelter. Similarly, when women are leaving such temporary shelters, the social workers must once again prepare them with realistic expectations for life outside.

The following example shows how crucial this particular intervention is to the well-being of the client.

> **Case Details:** Hira, a 31-year-old housewife, had come to the Special Cell due to intolerable physical, emotional and sexual harassment from her husband. She had tried to run away from home before, but her husband had traced her and brought her back. Neither her natal nor marital families were in a position to support her. When Hira managed to run away and come to the Special Cell, she requested to be away from her husband's clutches. She needed to distance herself physically from the violent situation till she recovered her physical and psychological health, which had been completely eroded due to the violence.
>
> **Intervention:** The Special Cell worker arranged to place Hira in a shelter home where she could have peace and solitude, but could remain in touch with the worker via telephone and occasional visits. The worker also arranged for a medical checkup and treatment. After she had somewhat recovered, Hira expressed a desire to work and be economically independent. The worker arranged for her discharge from the shelter home, after discussing with her the precautions to be taken while staying alone outside the safety of the shelter. The social worker helped her to find a job as a domestic worker. She began to earn adequately, got back in touch with her natal family, and ended up an emotionally stronger person to the point where she was able to deal with a later situation of sexual harassment on her own.

Working With Men in the Interest of Violated Women

Social workers at the Special Cells are trained to engage men in the attempt to reduce domestic violence in the home. One of the ways in which they may do so, is to use a Call Letter to request the man who is perpetrating the violence to visit the Cell. If there is no response to the Call Letter, they make a home visit. If the home visit also fails to elicit a response, they seek the help of the police to call the perpetrator to the Special Cell.

During the initial contact with the male perpetrator in an individual meeting, the worker expresses interest in hearing the man's side of the story and listens to his perception of the problem without voicing the woman's grievance or trying to confront him. Subsequently, the worker uses the strategy of explaining the imbalance of power in gender relations and verbally challenges his misuse of this power. The social worker helps the abuser to face his violent behaviour. She informs him about the legal rights of the violated woman and attempts to initiate change in his violent behaviour. Sometimes, the social worker has to expose the hollowness of the man's arguments by reversing it in such a way that he cannot help but acknowledge the imbalance.

The Special Cell worker also asks questions about the perpetrator's mental, sexual and social health and, when necessary, encourages him to seek treatment. For instance, if the perpetrator is addicted to alcohol or other substances, he is first motivated to and then assisted in seeking treatment. The social worker will also strive to build support systems to sustain behavioural and attitudinal change in him in the interest of the violated woman by negotiating with his family, employer and other stakeholders.

Social work interventions related to working with men are not limited to working with the perpetrator of violence but also involves working with men in both the natal and matrimonial families of the violated woman, as well as with other stakeholders, including the police to enlist their support for her.

The first case illustration shows how a simple intervention involving helping the man to attend to his physical health, helped to improve the marital relationship. In the second case illustration, the social worker had to work to help the husband accept that his wife had needs and to make space for this. The third case shows how the social worker had to work hard to break through the faulty arguments of the perpetrator using humour and reality orientation.

Case 1

Case details: Rita experienced physical and mental abuse from the husband immediately after marriage, and within 15 days of marriage, was sent back to her natal house. When she came to the Special Cell, she said that she wanted to be united with her husband.

Intervention: The husband, who was based in another district, did not respond to Call Letters, and the social worker sought the help of the police to persuade him to attend a meeting at the Special Cell. During the course of this meeting, the social worker discovered that the marriage had not been consummated and that the husband was infected with a sexually transmitted disease. Thus the worker persuaded him to seek treatment for his medical problem before undertaking the process for reconciliation.

Case 2

Case Details: Seema, who was a young wife, was finding it difficult to tolerate the excessive preoccupation of her marital family regarding certain religious rituals–the family believed that the mother-in-law was 'possessed' by a female deity and they, along with other community members, would gather to worship her. This situation created an additional work burden for Seema and placed various restrictions on her. This compounded a communication problem between the couple and led to their estrangement. Seema approached the Special Cell for help.

Intervention: The social worker helped the husband to understand that he needed to make space for his wife, to enable her to express her religious beliefs in her own way.

The social worker used the technique of contracting (which is used in cases of marital discord where the goal is reconciliation–it is used to alter certain modes of behaviour such as communication patterns, to deal with alcoholism, or to ensure regular visits to a psychiatrist). She brokered an understanding between the couple as to the extent to which Seema would participate in these religious rituals and the exact tasks for which she would be responsible. The couple agreed that if they found it difficult to communicate certain things verbally to each other, they would at least communicate through telephone, SMS, or written messages on chits, on the condition that they said at least one positive thing to each other each day. They also agreed to report to the Special Cell at specified intervals.

Case 3

Case details: Usha, aged 39 years, faced verbal abuse from her husband, Umesh and his family because she could not have children. He threatened to kill her. Fed up with the harassment, she went to stay with her natal family. At this time, she discovered she had a tumour in her uterus. Her husband was also asked to undergo medical tests and was found to have a low sperm count. Usha underwent a hysterectomy but her husband refused to bear the medical expenses or to look after her. At this point, Usha approached the Special Cell to make her marital family accept her back in their home.

Intervention: At the meeting with Umesh, he expressed reluctance to accept the client back because she had removed her uterus without his consent. The social worker explained to him that the hysterectomy was a medical necessity. When Umesh said that his family was not willing to accept Usha as she was now incapable of having a child, he was reminded that she was his wife and his responsibility, and that her medical problem was not her fault. Next Umesh accused Usha's family of keeping him in the dark regarding her health problem, and of getting her married without first giving her medical treatment. The social worker was successfully able to reverse the situation and make him see Usha's side of this picture by demonstrating that a similar situation could easily arise between his sister and her in-laws. She also confronted him with his own sperm count report and asked him if Usha would be justified in leaving him if she was capable of childbearing and he was not. At the second meeting, Umesh made a conditional change–to which Usha could return provided she did not oppose his second marriage. He expressed the need for a second marriage for the continuity of his family name. The Special Cell worker then demonstrated to Umesh in a jocular way the hollowness of such ideas, by probing his family history and making him realise that he did not know the names of his ancestors beyond his grandfather. She suggested the option of adoption to him and explained that given his medical history, he may not have a child even through a second marriage. At the third meeting, Umesh was willing to take Usha back. The social worker, at this point, had to work on changing the attitudes of Usha's father-in-law, who was opposed to the idea and wanted the couple to stay separately. The social worker made the father understand that Usha can exercise her right to stay in the marital home in spite of his opposition; however, his graceful consent would ensure cordial relations between them in future. He was assured that any of the parties could approach the Cell in case of further conflicts.

Re-establishment of Women's Relationship with their Economic Assets

Women survivors of domestic abuse often face financial violence, as their partners, in-laws and natal family often use control over economic resources to keep them subjugated. Part of the recovery process involves restoring the economic rights that are denied to these women. As part of the intervention, the social worker makes efforts to identify details of the economic assets of the woman's family, as the woman herself may be in the dark.

The Special Cell worker makes the woman, her family and other stakeholders aware of her economic rights such as her right to streedhan, inheritance, property, housing, maintenance as well as her right to be included in crucial documents such as ration cards, licenses and wills. The worker also assists her in her efforts to secure these rights. Negotiating with the perpetrators and others to ensure the payment of dues to the violated woman forms an important part of the intervention of the Special Cells. The social worker also encourages and tries to assist the woman to be economically independent.

Case 1

Case details: Sheena's husband was a chronic alcoholic and did not fulfill his financial responsibilities to the family. Sheena also suffered physical violence from him and his family. Tired of life, she attempted suicide. Her marital family threw her out of the house. Sheena went back to her natal home where her elder brother began fighting with her and pressuring her to leave the house. Sheena turned to the Special Cell to intervene and help recover her streedhan.

Intervention: The Special Cell worker started negotiations with Sheena's marital family for her streedhan. The social worker also explained to Sheena's brother that she had a right to stay in their father's house. Since the brother was staying in a separate house, he was asked not to interfere. After a few months, Sheena came to the Special Cell with a complaint of physical abuse by her brother. The worker called a joint meeting with her father and her brother. They both refused to allow Sheena to reside in the house. Sheena's natal family owned a paan shop. Sheena requested to be allowed to run the paan shop and to be permitted to stay in the shop. Her brother agreed to this arrangement as well as to pay the rent for the shop, provided Sheena paid the electricity bill. Sheena agreed to this and was able to officially add her name to the electricity bill. In time, Sheena also successfully recovered her streedhan. Ten years later, Sheena dropped by the Special Cell to inform the social worker that her father had died and that the shop was now fully owned by her.

Developmental Counselling with Violated Women

After helping the woman deal with the immediate crisis in her life, the Special Cell social worker encourages her to become more aware, more confident and better equipped to deal with new challenges that she might encounter. This forms a part of developmental counselling, wherein the woman survivor is enabled to grow emotionally, physically and mentally to meet current and future challenges. The social worker educates her about her rights, helps her to enhance her educational qualifications and encourages her to become economically independent through identifying opportunities for employment.

Many survivors who access the Special Cells shoulder the responsibility of raising their children on their own. Development counselling is critical to preparing them for this task. One practical step that social workers take is to advise mothers who are eligible, to obtain a caste certificate, which help their children to secure facilities under reservation such as admission in school and concessions on expenditure.

In another practical measure, women who have married into families which own land are assisted in protecting the inheritance of their children by ensuring that their children's names are mentioned in the *saat baara ka utara* – a document of legal significance which is maintained by the State Revenue Department and which indicates among other details ownership of agricultural land and land that has been converted into non-agricultural land.

Case 2

Case details: Nafisa, an eighteen-year-old girl from a lower middle-class Muslim family, who had completed senior secondary education came to the Special Cell for help. Her husband, who was much older than her, habitually abused her physically and mentally, and had finally thrown her out of their marital home. Neither was Nafisa willing to go back to her abusive husband, nor was her husband interested in her doing so, but her natal family was pressuring her to reconcile on the grounds that three of her sisters were yet to be married.

Intervention: The social worker met with the natal family and convinced them that the relationship would not work if both partners were unwilling and that Nafisa should not be compelled to return to her abusive marriage. The social worker then negotiated with the husband to return her streedhan and to provide maintenance. At this point, the couple decided to get divorced.

During individual meetings with Nafisa, the social worker discovered that she was keen to pursue her education and was good at academics. Since Nafisa's family was conservative and would not permit her to attend a regular co-ed college, the social worker gathered information about colleges for Muslim girls that offered vocational education. By then Nafisa had obtained her divorce and had entered her *iddat* period where by custom, Muslim women undergoing a divorce are not permitted to leave the house or meet any males with whom they can forge a marital relationship.

The social worker visited her home during this iddat period to meet her and keep motivating her, as well as to convince her family to permit her to continue her education and gain financial independence.

During these home visits, the social worker discovered that Nafisa's grandfather was more progressive in his thinking than the rest of her family and so she enlisted his help in influencing other family members. The outcome was that Nafisa enrolled for vocational training. Further, the Special Cell worker ensured that the maintenance she received as a lump sum was invested in a bank fixed deposit in her name.

Advocacy for Group Entitlement in the Interest of Violated Women

The areas of intervention by the Special Cell described up to this point relate to individual cases. However, a very important area of work for the Special Cells pertains to advocacy, outreach and building awareness regarding violence against women.

Here, the Special Cells aim to promote acceptance in society of the woman's inalienable human rights, give visibility to the issue of violence against women, and highlight society's responsibility to end such violence. To this end, the Special Cell social workers engage with various fora and networks. They proactively respond to various related initiatives of the state and the voluntary sector. The Special Cells organise training programmes for police, members of civil services and members of the judiciary, participate in programmes organised by other institutions, and conduct awareness programmes in communities and educational institutions, along with interacting with media personnel, to bring visibility to issues of violence against women. Through their routine interactions with police officials, bureaucrats, lawyers, magistrates, Protection Officers, *mahila mandals,* jaat panchayats, village panchayats, religious organisations and youth groups, they present consistent messages about not tolerating violence against women.

In conclusion, one can say, the interventions at the Special Cell are multi-pronged, and aim not only to alleviate crisis situations, but also empower women and address wider questions of inequality and power. The social worker is located at a critical juncture – in the interface with the client, perpetrator, system and community. Feminist social work intervention practice thus emphasises the need to address systemic as well as individual imbalances and violence, and preserves the fundamental right of a woman to a violence free life.

The monitoring indicators that guide the interventions at the Cells often overlap in implementation yet provide clarity in determining how the non-negotiable principles of the Special Cells' work may be realised in practice. Social workers must be resourceful in adapting to and addressing the varied needs of the Cells' client, and this review of cases demonstrates the innovation and creative problem-solving that must be undertaken in order to provide redressal and support to women survivors.

Voices of Change: Testimonies from Survivors and Stakeholders

THIS CHAPTER HIGHLIGHTS the impact of the Special Cells on the lives of individuals, and, through their own voices and narratives, provides insight into this decade of work and the experiences of the people involved. It includes testimonies from ex-clients, personnel from the Cells and a police official.

An ever-present theme in these testimonies is change. Client testimonies, from ex-clients who were willing to share their experiences at the Cells, address not only the changes in their life situation that came about as a result of the interventions from the Special Cells, but also the transformation in their personality, particularly a new-found confidence to live life on their own terms. These narratives highlight the advantage of the location of the Special Cell within the police system and of intervention strategies such as home visits and individual meetings with the perpetrator. They show that change may not always be in the direction anticipated by the client, but that the lives of survivors who reach the Special Cells are never the same. Client's names have been changed to preserve confidentiality.

Social workers associated with the Special Cells in the past and at present also testify that their lives changed because of their work in this service context, and speak about the evolution and developments in their thoughts and understandings about violence against women, and their growing confidence in engaging with the system. We approached social workers who had worked in the Special Cells between 2003 and 2012, and the narratives we received highlight and document the journey of the programme, as well as the myriad personal journeys and evolutions that accompanied it.

The final testimonial, a fitting note to end with, comes from a police official who witnessed the journey of expansion, in varied roles, over this decade. He sheds light on how, at the systemic level, the Special Cells have been effective in creating change in policies, procedures and in the perspective of people who are part of the system.

Survivors' Stories

Case 1

पहिल्यांदा मी महिला सहाय्य कक्षात गेले तो दिवस मला अजूनही आठवतो. खूप टेन्शन होते, जाऊ का नको वाटत होते. हिम्मत करून मी आत गेले. पण जेव्हा तिथल्या कार्यकर्त्यांबरोबर मी बोलले, तेव्हा मला कमालीचं बरं वाटलं. खूप relaxed वाटलं. असं वाटलं I have reached my destination.

त्यांनी मला समोरच्या देवळात बसून अर्ज लिहायला सांगितला. किती लिहू आणि किती नाही असं मला झालं होतं. अर्ज लिहिल्यावर त्यांनी मला अगदी शांतपणे समजुन घेतले व समजावूनही सांगितले.मला भरपूर वेळ दिला. त्यांच्याशी बोलल्यानंतर मला पंख फुटल्यासारखे छान वाटत होते. असं वाटत होतं कि स्त्री ही कमजोर नाही. ती

सगळे काही करू शकते. आणि आजपर्यंत त्यांनी दिलेल्या विश्वासाने, हिमतीने मी सगळे व्यवस्थित करते आहे.

कक्षामधून मला mental support खूप मिळाला. माझे त्यांच्याबरोबर नाते एवढे strong build झाले होते, की केव्हाही अडचण आली कि मी त्यांना फोन करायची. केव्हाही insecure झाले कि रात्री दोन वाजता सुद्धा मी त्यांना फोन करत असे. सख्खे नातेवाईक सुद्धा एवढे कुणासाठी करत नाहीत.

मी अशा कुटुंबामधून आहे जिथे कोर्ट, कचेरी, पोलिस हे शब्द महिलांनाच काय पुरुषांना सुद्धा लांब लांबपर्यंत माहित नाहीत. माझा परिवार आहे त्यांना हे कुठेतरी बुद्धीला पटत नव्हतं. कितीही त्रास झाला तरी आपले संस्कार आहेत, आपले नाव आहे, इज्जत आहे, ती सांभाळायची, आपण सहन करायचे आणि राहायचे नवऱ्याबरोबर. पण हे कुठपर्यंत? मी ठरवलं कि आता आपण याच्यातून बाहेर पडायचे आणि मी महिला सहाय्य कक्षात आले.

हिम्मत तर माझ्यात लहानपणापासून आहे पण अशी हिम्मत करणे ही खूप मोठी, खूप वेगळी गोष्ट आहे. हे कुठेतरी समाजाला रुचत नाही. त्यांना divorce घेणे ही एक भयानक गोष्ट वाटते. पण मी ठरवले, आपल्याला समाजाशी काही देणे घेणे नाही. शेवटी आपले आयुष्य आहे. माझी मुले मोठी होत चालली होती. मला हे violence थांबवायचे होते. शेवटी मी निर्णय घेतला. हा निर्णय घेण्याआधी दहा बारा दिवस मी खूप विचार केला. मुलांना घेऊन वेगळे राहण्याचा आपण आज निर्णय घेतला, तर उद्या सकाळी उठल्यापासून रात्री झोपेपर्यंत आपल्या ज्या गरजा असतात; उठल्याबरोबर लागणारे साधी toothbrush आणि toothpaste घेण्यासाठी सुद्धा आपल्याकडे पैसे नाहीत. तर आपण ही हिम्मत करावी का? पण हा हि विचार केला कि हा जो त्रास आहे - त्याचे घरातून निघून जाणे, कर्ज, आणखी बऱ्याचशा गोष्टी होत्या- त्यातून मुक्त व्हायचे तर काही तरी करावेच लागणार. मग एका नव्या आयुष्याला सुरुवात केली. त्यात कक्षाचा मोठा वाटा आहे.

व्यक्ती म्हणून माझ्या आयुष्यात कक्षात आल्यावर झालेले बदल सांगायचे म्हटले तर माझ्या शब्दकोशात भीती हा शब्दच राहिलेला नाही. मला आता कसलीच भीती नाही. कक्षात आल्यावर माझ्या

आयुष्यात प्रचंड बदल झाला. माझा आत्मविश्वास वाढला, माझी body language बदलली, मला friend circle वाढवावसे वाटले. एखाद्या घरेलू बाईला पुरुषाशी बोलायला खूप hesitation होतं. तसं hesitation मला राहिलं नाही- जे आधी होतं. बाहेर पडलं कि स्त्री पुरुष दोघे समान असतात. बघणाऱ्यांना काय वाटेल तो मी कधीच विचार करत नाही. आपल्याला वाटत असेल कि जग बदलावं तर आधी आपण बदललं पाहिजे. मी तेच केलं.

आज माझा प्रश्न मिटला आहे, फारकत झाली आहे. मी अत्यंत आनंदी आणि यशस्वी आयुष्य जगते आहे. तरी अजूनही मी कक्षाच्या संपर्कात आहे. कारण पहिल्यापासून मला इथल्या कार्यकर्त्यांनी त्यांचे designation कधीच जाणवू दिले नाही. मी एक 'client' आहे असं वागविले नाही. एक friendly वातावरण तयार केले. मी त्या दिवसापासून कार्यकर्त्यांना एक friend च समजते.

जेव्हा माझी family court त केस गेली, तेव्हा मी खूप depression मध्ये होते. मला वकील चांगले मिळाले नव्हते.त्यांच्या assistant ची भाषा योग्य नव्हती. माझी खूप चिडचिड व्हायची. टेन्शन यायच. तेव्हा मला वाटे कक्षाचे कार्यकर्ते सुद्धा तिथे हवे होते. ते असते तर एक moral support मिळाला असता. त्यांच्या कामाची सीमा एका जिल्ह्यापुरती मर्यादित असते. माझे यजमान दुसऱ्या जिल्ह्यात होते तिथे तेव्हा कक्ष नव्हता. ती एक barrier होती. तुमच्या कक्षात येणाऱ्या महिलांना छळणाऱ्या पुरुषांना शिक्षा देण्याचा अधिकार तुम्हाला असायला हवा असं मला प्रामाणिकपणे वाटतं.

मी माझ्या mobile मध्ये कक्षातील कार्यकर्त्यांचे नाव save केले आहे ना, तिथे एक दिपक ठेवला आहे. माझ्या आयुष्यात त्यांनी या दिपकाचे काम केले आहे.

I still remember the first day at the Special Cell, I had approached it with a lot of tension and apprehension, but when I came out I was relaxed and felt I had reached my destination. I was given a lot of support.

I came from a family where no one approaches any outside agency like police, court for the women facing violence.

Women are supposed to bear everything and not complain to anybody. Divorce is very unthinkable in our society, but after facing so much of violence along with my children, I decided that I had to stop this. I did face some difficulty when my case was in the Family Court and wished that the social workers of Special Cell were there with me.

Now after coming to the Special Cell I am a changed person, I have become very confident, fearless and my body language has changed. I have a large friends' circle. I have started believing that if you have to change the world around, you have to bring a change in yourself. The Special Cell workers are like friends and have been like a lamp who have guided me.

—Saroj Nashikkar

Case 2

मी व माझे सध्याचे पती आठ-नऊ महिने एकत्र राहत होतो. राहिलो याच पद्धतीने की next month मध्ये लग्न करूया. पण आमचे खूप प्रोब्लेम्स होते, त्यांच्यावर financial केसेस चालू होत्या. ते नेहमी लग्नासाठी टाळाटाळ करत होते. शेवटी आम्ही ठरविले कि दसऱ्याच्या मुहूर्तावर आपण मंदिरात का असेना लग्न करून आपले relation पुढे नेऊ. पण ठरलेल्या वेळी, ठरलेल्या जागी ते आलेच नाहीत. मला खूप राग आला त्या गोष्टीचा, म्हणून मी पोलिस स्टेशनला complaint करायला गेले. त्यांनी मला suggest केले की तुम्ही तक्रार करून काहीच होणार नाही. म्हणजे त्यांना जी शिक्षा मिळायची असेल ती मिळेल पण तुम्ही Women Cell मध्ये जाऊन बघा. तुम्हाला व्यवस्थित वाटले तर तुम्ही counselling घ्या. त्याच्यामुळे कदाचित तुमचे चांगले होईल.

दुसऱ्या दिवशी मी Cell मध्ये गेले. तिथे गेल्यावर Madam ने मला समजावले की इथे दोघांची बाजू ऐकून घेतली जाणार. इथे complaint होत नाही. जो काही निर्णय असेल तो तुम्हाला दोघांना स्वतंत्रपणे घ्यायचा आहे.मला योग्य वाटले. नंतर मी application दिले. त्यांना बोलाविल्यावरही त्यांनी टाळाटाळ केले. पण Madam ने थोडे strictly फोन करून सांगितले की तुम्ही आला नाहीत तर पोलिसांची मदत

घ्यावी लागेल, म्हणून ते थोडे serious झाले. त्यांच्याबरोबर meeting साठी त्यांना कक्षात बोलावले, पण ते तरीपण मला सोबत Cell मध्ये घेऊन आले. Madam ने मला बाहेरच बसवले. त्यांनी मला strictly सांगितले की मला ह्यांच्याशीच बोलायचे आहे. त्यांना गोष्ट कळाली की हिच्याशी जर त्या एकटयामध्ये बोलतात तर माझ्याशी पण एकटयामध्येच बोलतील. त्यांना कळाले की इथे भेदभाव होत नाही. त्यांची पण तेवढीच बाजू ऐकून घेतली जाते. तेव्हापासून Madam चा ते खूप respect करतात.

दोन-तीन मिटिंग झाल्यानंतर त्यांनी मान्य केले की लग्न करेन. पण लग्नानंतरही ते distance ठेवायचे. मी त्यांच्या लग्नाची बायको असूनसुद्धा त्यांनी मला Facebook मध्ये block ठेवले होते. Madam ने माझ्यासोबत single meeting केली. त्यामध्ये त्यांनी सांगितले की तुझ्या personal growth कडे लक्ष दे. स्वतःकडे लक्ष दे. बायको झाल्यानंतर माझा हक्क म्हणूनही माझ्या यजमानांनी कधीही त्यांचा पगार मला सांगितला नाही. ते जुगार खेळायचे, त्यामुळे त्यांनी बरेच पैसे घेतले होते. त्यांच्या कर्जदाराचे मला फोन यायचे. मला खूप harass करायचे. म्हणून Madam ने मला त्यांचे फोन घेऊ नये असे सांगितले. Madam ने त्यांना त्यांची भूमिका काय आहे समजावले. मी जेव्हा Special Cell मध्ये गेली तेव्हा खूप depressed होती. माझा confidence low होता. माझ्या पतीसोबत रहान होते तेंव्हा त्यांनी माझा confidence खूप कमी केलेला होता. Special Cell ने माझा confidence वाढवला.

मला वाटते की जर मी Special Cell ला आली नसती तर माझे पती त्यांच्या वागण्यावर ठाम राहिले असते. अजूनही त्यांनी तेच केले असते. खरं तर माझ्या घरचे सर्व ह्यांना घाबरायचे. कारण हा माणूस खूप violent आहे. हा मारझोड करतो. मला म्हणायचे तू त्याच्याबरोबर नको जाऊ. Cell मध्ये आल्यानंतर माझ्या घरचे पण एकदम बदलले. आज मी खूप समाधानी आहे. आज तसं काही नाही. पहिले ते माझ्याकडे लक्ष द्यायचे नाही. पण आता मला हवं नको ते विचारतात. आता आम्ही बेबी साठी पण plan करतो आहोत.

Actually काय असते की आपण खूप घाईत असतो. माझ्यासोबत असे झाले आहे, म्हणून मला आताच्या आत्ता justice मिळाला पाहिजे.

मला समजले की घाई करून चालत नाही. घाई करून गोष्टी बिघडू शकतात. मी खरं सांगते सुरुवातीला मला वाटायचे की Special Cell मध्ये दोन महिन्यानंतर meeting साठी बोलावतात. कधी single meeting, कधी joint meeting एवढा वेळ का घालवतात? पण आता कळते की तो वेळ खूप महत्वाचा असतो. त्या दोन महिन्यामध्ये एकमेकांविषयी खूप गोष्टी कळतात. एकमेकांशी कसे वागायचे, बोलायचे हे समजते.

Madam ने मला खूप समजून घेतले. त्यांनी आम्हाला दोघानाही ऐकून घेतले. आज पण मी त्यांना म्हटले की Madam ने appointment दिली आहे. मला जायचे आहे. मी ट्रेन ने येणार होती पण त्यांनी मला स्वतः इथे गाडीने सोडले. ते मला म्हणाले माझ्या colleague विषयी पण बोल. तिला पण violence आहे. मी माझ्या मैत्रिणीला Cell विषयी सांगितले, कारण तिला तिचा नवरा मारझोड करत होता. Counselling मुळे फरक पडतो. इथे आल्यावर त्यांना कायदा समजतो. Special Cell प्रत्येक पोलिस ठाण्यात असायलाच हवे. अर्ध्या पेक्षा जास्त पुरुष तर बायकांना हेच सांगतात की तू एक स्त्री आहेस; जर तू बाहेर गेली तर तुझ्याबरोबर वाईट होऊ शकते. त्यांचा confidence इतका low करतात कि त्या कधी पोलिस स्टेशन ची पायरी नाही चढणार. Open ground मध्ये आपण बायकांसाठी awareness programmes ठेवले पाहिजे.

कक्षात आल्यानंतर जो माझा purpose होता लग्न करण्याचा तो fulfil झाला आहे. मी स्वतः खूप स्वतंत्र झाली आहे. माझ्या मते तरी Violence पूर्णपणे zero झालेला आहे. आजच्या date मध्ये पण जर त्यांनी मला सांगितले की आपण वेगळे होऊया तर मी त्यांना विचारेन की आपण कधीपासून वेगळे व्हायचे आहे. हा स्वतःबद्दलचा आत्मविश्वास वाढलेला आहे. Thank you Special Cell!

I was in a live-in relationship with my present husband for past 6-7months. Due to some problems, our final marriage was getting postponed. We had decided to get married on Dussera Day, but my partner did not come to the venue. I was very angry and went to the Police Station to complain but they directed me to the Special Cell for interventions. Next day, I went to the Special Cell where a social worker gave a orientation talk about how the Cell works.

The Social Worker had individual and joint meetings with both of us. I understood the importance of process-oriented work. With the intervention of the Special Cell, I and my partner got married, but violence continued even after marriage, and we both went back to the Special Cell for intervention.

Now I have become a more confident person, there is no violence in this relationship. My husband and family have become more caring. I have so much confidence that now I can manage everything independently. I feel that there should be a Special Cell in every Police Station.

—**Neena**

Case 3

मी एका Catholic family मधून आले आहे. माझं arranged marriage झालं होतं. लग्नानंतर हळूहळू मला कळलं कि माझा नवरा काहीच करत काम नाही. मलाही काम सोडायला लावलं होतं. मला एक रुपया सुद्धा खर्चाला मिळत नव्हता. घरातल्या कुठल्याही decision मध्ये मला involve करत नव्हते , नवरा फक्त आई बोलेल ते ऐकायचा. सगळं बोलणं English मध्ये चालायचे , जे मला समजत नव्हतं. आमचं husband-wife असं काही relation च नव्हतं. तो मला काहीच time देत नव्हता.

माझे सासरे चांगले होते, पण ते लग्नानंतर लगेच गेले आणि या लोकांचा त्रास अजून वाढला. माझ्या घरचे लोकं पण माझी side घेत नव्हते. माझा भाऊ म्हणाला त्रास सहन कर पण त्या घरातून बाहेर नाही पडायचं. मला काही रस्ताच नाही राहिला. खूप depression आलं तेव्हा मी जीव द्यायचा प्रयत्न केला. त्यातून मी वाचले, पण मग ह्या लोकांनी म्हटलं कि हिला आता घरात ठेवणार नाही. मी म्हटलं मग divorce द्या. पण आम्ही Catholic. माझा नवरा divorce द्यायला तयार नव्हता आणि घरचे सुद्धा मला divorce साठी support करत नव्हते. माझ्या एका friend ची बाजूवाली संस्थेत काम करते. तिला Cell बद्दल

माहिती होती. म्हणून मी २०१० मध्ये divorce साठी मदत मागायला Cell मध्ये गेले. Cell मधून पत्र पाठवल्यावर नवरा आला नाही. मग Madam त्याच्या घरी गेल्या तेव्हा आला, पण divorce द्यायला साफ मना केलं. मग Madam ने मला वकिलाकडे पाठविले. Madam ने वकिलाला सगळी माहिती दिली, मला जास्त खर्च पडू नये यासाठी मदत केली. मला जेव्हा जेव्हा काही problem यायचा तेव्हा तेव्हा मी Cell ला जायची. ५ वर्षांनंतर मला divorce मिळाला. Madam च्या मदती शिवाय, Cell च्या मदतीशिवाय divorce मिळणं एक impossible गोष्ट होती. माझ्याकडे रेशन कार्ड नव्हतं. ते मिळवायला मला Cell ने मदत केली.

सुरुवातीला मी जेव्हा Cell ला आले, तेव्हा मला माझ्या problem बद्दल बोलायची लाज वाटायची. नवऱ्याबरोबर संबंध नाही हे सांगणे घाणेरडे, लाजिरवाणे वाटे. इथे आल्यावर कळले, असे संबंध असणे हा माझा हक्क आहे. आधी मी खूप घाबरायची. आता कसली भीती नाही. कक्षात येऊन हा आत्मविश्वास आला. साध्या माणसांना कायदा माहित नसतो. यांच्या मुळे मला कायदा कळला. हिम्मत मिळाली. बाईला थोडीशी हिम्मत द्यायची गरज असते. मग पुढली खटपट ती स्वत: करू शकते.

मला कधीपण काही problem आला, तर मी Cell ला यायचे. मला इथून काही न काही मदत मिळेल असा मला विश्वास वाटायचा आणि मला नेहमीच इथून मदत मिळायची. इथून मदत मिळाली नाही तरी सही मार्ग दिसतो. एकदा लग्न झालं, कि घराचे हात वर करतात. मुलीला बोझ समजतात. मी इकडे आले तेव्हा मला वाटलं, आता मी बिन आसऱ्याची नाही. जेव्हा मला divorce मिळाला, तेव्हा कोर्टातून मी direct Cell ला गेले, घरी सुद्धा गेले नाही कारण ही आनंदाची बातमी मला Madam च्याबरोबर share करायची होती. मला वाटलं माझ्या आनंदात यांचाही हक्क आहे.

आता मी Job ला जाते. आपलं आपण कमावून खाते. त्या माणसाच्या हाताखालून सुटले, याचा मला आनंद आहे. आमची गावाला सामायिक जमीन आहे. मी सांगितले आहे माझा त्यातला वाटा मला द्या. मला तिथे घर बांधून राहायचे आहे. Life मध्ये परत partner करेन का नाही माहित नाही पण घर नक्की करेन हक्काचं. Depend नाही

राहणार कोणावर. तसं माझं परदेशात जायचं स्वप्न आहे. Passport साठी apply केलं आहे. Problem मिटला तरी मी Cell च्या Contact मध्ये असते. Madam ना भेटायला येते. बुरे वक्त में जिन्होने साथ दिया उन्हे अच्छे वक्त में भी याद रखना चाहिये!

I am from a catholic family. I had an arranged marriage. Few months into marriage I realised that my husband was unemployed. I started facing violence from my husband and matrimonial family. They started isolating me. My husband and matrimonial family would communicate in English which I could not follow. My father-in-law was supportive but he expired soon after my marriage. There was no support from my natal family, I went into depression and tried committing suicide, but was saved.

I was driven out of my matrimonial home when I told my husband I wanted a divorce. He refused to give me a divorce, saying that Catholics do not divorce and his view was supported by my natal family.

I got to know of the Special Cell from my friends in the neighbourhood. I approached the Special Cell to help me get a divorce from my husband. A Call Letter was sent to my husband but he did not come, so the social worker paid a home visit to convince him to visit the Special Cell. In the Special Cell also he refused to give me a divorce, so I was referred for legal support to a lawyer and I got divorce from my husband after a struggle of 5 years in the court.

When I had first approached the Special Cell, I used to feel ashamed. There was a lot of self- blame. I used to feel ashamed of talking of sexual violence but later on understood that living a violence-free life was my right. For any and all problems in my life I soon began to approach the Special Cell. They are always supportive and if they cannot find any solution themselves, they refer me to concerned agency.

Now I am confident, independent, working. I am happy that I am out of the abusive relationship. I have also started asking for my rights in my natal home. I have plans to go abroad to earn. But I will always stay in touch with the social workers of the Special Cell.

—Neha

Social Workers' Stories

Voice 1

टाटा सामाजिक विज्ञान संस्थेच्या 'महिला व मुलांकरिता सहाय्य कक्ष' या उपक्रमासोबतचे कार्य हा माझ्या आयुष्याला नवी दिशा देणारा अनुभव होता. महिला सहाय्य कक्षाची विचारसरणी व कामकाजामुळेच माझा पुरुषत्वापासून माणुसकीकडे जाणारा प्रवास सुरु झाला.

दि १४ फेब्रुवारी २००३ रोजी महिला व मुलांकरिता सहाय्य कक्ष नांदेड ची स्थापना पोलीस अधीक्षक कार्यालयात झाली. महिलाविषयक प्रश्नांना दिल्या जाणाऱ्या दुय्यम वागणुकीचा प्रत्यय पहिल्याच दिवशी कक्ष कार्यकर्त्यांना आला, कारण कक्षाला कार्यालयाऐवजी झाडाखाली मोडलेले टेबल व खुर्ची घेवून कामकाज सुरु करावे लागले. कक्षासमोर साधन सामुग्रीचा अभाव, जागेचा अभाव ही आव्हाने कधीच नवी नव्हती, असेल त्या परिस्थितीत व उपलब्ध साधनातून कक्षाने कामकाज सुरु केले. कक्षासमोर आव्हान एकच होते आणि ते म्हणजे पोलीस खाते व समाजातील पुरुष प्रधान मानसिकता, त्याला उपाय होता कक्षाची विचारधारा. कक्षाच्या विचारधारेच्या सहाय्याने आम्ही कार्य सुरु केले व वाढवले.

सर्वप्रथम आम्ही पोलीस अधीक्षक कार्यालयातील प्रत्येक विभागात माणसे जोडली व त्यांच्यासोबत महिलाविषयक प्रश्नावर संवाद सुरु केला. त्यामुळे कार्यालयात कक्षाची वेगळी ओळख बनण्यास सुरुवात झाली. जिल्ह्यातील ३५ पोलीस स्टेशनांना आम्ही भेट दिली. पोलीस स्टेशन पातळीवरील महिला सुरक्षा समिती व जिल्हा स्तरावरील महिला तक्रार निवारण समितीसोबत बैठका घेण्यात आल्या व जिल्हाभर एक नेटवर्क निर्माण करण्याचा आम्ही प्रयत्न केला. पोलीस

प्रशिक्षण, जाणीव जागृती कार्यक्रमांच्या माध्यमातून महिला विषयक प्रश्नांवर पोलीस खात्याच्या माध्यमातून न्याय मिळवून देण्याचा प्रयत्न सुरु झाला.

कक्षाच्या कार्याची दखल घेवून पोलीस अधीक्षक नांदेड यांनी कक्ष कार्यकर्त्यांना जिल्हास्तरावरील महिला तक्रार निवारण समितीवर सदस्य म्हणून निवड करून कार्य करण्याची संधी दिली.त्यामुळे कक्षाचे कामकाज प्रभावीपणे मांडण्यास खूपच मदत झाली.

कक्षाने जिल्हास्तरावर होणाऱ्या महिला अत्याचाराच्या गंभीर गुन्ह्यावर लक्ष ठेवण्यास सुरुवात केली व घटना स्थळी भेट देवून पोलीस स्टेशनस्तरावर सदर गुन्ह्याबाबत चर्चा करण्यास सुरुवात केली. परिणामतः स्थानिक पातळीवर पोलीस स्टेशन महिला विषयक गुन्ह्याचा गंभीरपणे तपास करू लागले व महिला विषयक प्रश्नांची दखल घेवू लागले. पोलीस अधीक्षक कार्यालय नांदेडला पोलीस व प्रशिक्षित सामाजिक कार्यकर्ते यांचे स्वतंत्र पथक तयार झाले व एकमेकांच्या सहकार्याने महिला विषयक प्रश्नांवर कार्य करू लागले. कक्षाच्या कार्यक्षमतेची प्रचिती येऊ लागल्यावर नांदेड पोलीसांची महिला तक्रार निवारण समिती व TISS चे महिला कक्ष यांना कार्यालायासाठी नवीन इमारतीत स्वतंत्र जागा मिळाली. तसेच आवश्यक फर्निचर व जिल्हा भेटीसाठी स्वतंत्र गाडी पोलीस अधीक्षक यांनी उपलब्ध करून दिली. ज्या पोलीस अधीक्षक कार्यालयात कक्षाला झाडाखाली सुरुवात करावी लागली त्याच कार्यालयात कक्षासाठी ७०० चौ.मी ची स्वतंत्र जागा मिळणे आम्हा सर्वासाठी अभिमानास्पद होते.

कक्षाचे कार्य विस्तारण्यासाठी पोलीस अधीक्षक नांदेड यांनी महिलांसाठी Helpline ची स्थापना केली. Helpline चे काम कक्षाच्या देखरेखीखाली सुरु झाले. यासाठी पोलीस दलातर्फे पोलीस कर्मचारी व कक्षाच्या वतीने स्वयंसेवक काम बघत होते. जिल्हाभरातून महिला Helpline ला फोन करुन विश्वासाने मदत मागू लागल्या. कक्षाच्या सामाजिक कार्यकर्त्यामुळे महिलांचे प्रश्न थेट पोलीस अधिक्षकापर्यंत पोहोचण्याचे व्यासपीठ निर्माण झाले.

कक्षाच्या विस्तारात कौटुंबिक हिंसाचारापासून महिलांचे संरक्षण कायदयाने देखिल महत्वपूर्ण योगदान दिले. कक्षाची सेवा पुखणारे

म्हणून झालेली निवड सार्थ ठरवण्यासाठी कक्षाने महिलांच्या तक्रारीवर कौटुंबिक हिंसाचार घटना अहवाल तयार करून प्रकरण न्यायालयात दाखल करण्याचे कार्य सुरु केले. या सर्व कार्याची दखल महाराष्ट्र राज्य महिला आयोगाच्या अध्यक्ष यांनी देखील घेवून कक्ष कार्यकर्त्यांना हिंगोली पोलीस अधीक्षक कार्यालयात नांदेड येथील धर्तीवर कार्य सुरु करण्यास सहकार्य मागितले ही देखील कक्षासाठी अभिमानाची बाब होती.

कक्षाचे वैशिष्ठ म्हणजे पुरुष व स्त्री कार्यकर्ते यांची team. माझ्या सहकारी श्रीमती ज्योती सपकाळे ह्यांचे या कामात महत्वपूर्ण योगदान आहे. कक्षाच्या या team च्या माध्यमातूनच हे कार्य शक्य झाले. मी व माझी सहकारी यांच्यामध्ये स्पर्धेची भावना कधीच नव्हती, होती ती सहकार्याची भावना. दोघांनी वैयक्तिक ध्येयाऐवजी कक्षाचे ध्येय महत्वाचे मानले व स्त्री-पुरुष कार्यकर्त्यापेक्षाही कक्ष कार्यकर्ते म्हणून आम्ही पोलीस विभागात वावरलो.

कक्षाची विचारधारा व कार्य यामुळे माझ्या वैयक्तिक विकासासाठी खूपच हातभार लागला. पुरुषापेक्षा माणूस म्हणून विकसित होणे महत्वाचे हा संदेश कक्ष स्थापनेच्या प्रवासातून अधोरेखीत झाला.

पितृसत्ताक समाजव्यवस्थेचा भाग असेलेला मी, महिला सहाय्य कक्षाचा भाग झाल्यानंतर सुरुवातीच्या काळात स्त्री-पुरुष समानतेबाबत मनात गोंधळलेलो होतो. कारण समानतेचा विचार तर स्वीकारायचा होता पण परंपरागत संस्कार कसे सोडायाचे हा प्रश्न होता. कधी कधी असे वाटायचे की स्त्री–पुरुष समानता ही न झेपणारी गोष्ट आहे. कक्षाच्या Gender Awareness programmes मध्ये सहभागी होऊन समाजिकीकरणाच्या प्रक्रीयेकडे Gender lens मधून पाहायला शिकलो आणि त्यामुळे पुढील वाटचाल सोपी झाली. महिलांवर होणारे अत्याचार हे साहजिक असतात हा विचाराचा प्रवाह किती चुकीचा आहे याची खऱ्या अर्थाने जाणीव झाली. स्त्री जन्मतःच दुय्यम नसून तिला दुय्यम बनविण्यामध्ये समाज, संस्कृती, रूढी परंपरा यांचा किती मोठा सहभाग आहे हे लक्षात यायला लागले. पुरुषांचा महिलांवरचा अत्याचार हा तिला नियंत्रणाखाली ठेवणे व आपण दुबळे/कमकुवत नाहीत हे निर्देश तिला देण्याकरिता असतात हे लक्षात आले, त्यामुळे मी पारंपारिक पुरुषी भूमिकेच्या

बाहेर जावून महिलांचे प्रश्न संवेदनशीलपणे हाताळायला शिकलो. या सर्व प्रक्रियेतून जाण्यामुळे मला माणूस म्हणून प्रगल्भ होण्यास व विकसित होण्यास निश्चितच खूप मदत झाली व त्यातून व्यावसायिक, कौटुंबिक व सामाजिक क्षेत्रात स्त्रियांना योग्य सन्मान व दर्जा द्यायला शिकलो.

महिलांवरील अत्याचार रोकण्यासाठी पुरुषांसोबत देखील काम करणे गरजेचे आहे असे मला वाटते कारण पितृसत्ताक समाजात पुरुषांची पण मानसिक पातळीवर कोंडी होत आहे, त्यांच्यामध्ये व्यक्त होण्याचे प्रमाण घटत आहे, मुळातच नकारात्मक भावना व्यक्त करायच्या नसतात असे संस्कार पुरुषांवर होतात त्यामुळे पुरुषांमध्ये व्यसनाचे प्रमाण वाढत आहे. पुरुषांना भावनाचे नियमन करण्याचे शिक्षण देण्याचीही खूप गरज आहे. कक्षाच्या व्यासपीठावरून स्त्री व पुरुष दोघांसोबत त्यांच्या कौटुंबिक व वैवाहिक प्रश्नावर काम करण्याची संधी मला मिळाली म्हणूनच आज मागे वळून पहिले तर असे जाणवते कि माझ्या पुरुषत्वाच्या प्रवासाला माणूसपणाकडे घेवून जाण्याचे काम महिला सहाय्य कक्षाने केले...!

Working with the Special Cell for women and children, implemented by Tata Institute of Social Sciences, was a life changing experience.

The Special Cell at Nanded started functioning from 14 February 2003 at the Superintendent of Police's Office. The first day was a revelation on how the police look at the issue of violence against women. We were given an office but that was taken away and we had to work under a tree. This was a challenge for the Cell, and an eye-opener on the patriarchal approach of the police and the larger society.

We started the work by networking with different stakeholders like personnel in the Police Station, the 'Mahila Suraksha Kaksh'. We were later on invited by the Superintendent of Police to be a member on the District Takrar Nivaran Kaksh, visiting the areas where the incidents had happened, this helped in understanding the intensity of violence against women which we then began discussing with the police. After that the police started investigating the cases of violence against women more effectively. As a result, a separate office was allocated to the Special Cell. To expand the work to curb Violence Against Women, a Helpline for women was started, in which both police personnel and the social workers handle cases with direct reporting to the Superintendent of Police.

The passing of the 'Protection of Women from Domestic Violence Act 2005' and the Special Cell being nominated as the 'service provider' helped in strengthening the work and linking violated women to the courts through filing of DIRs. The State Women's Commission also took note of the work.

The Special Cell had a team of female and male social workers. There was a good coordination between me and my colleague Jyoti Sapkale and this helped us in rendering assistance effectively to violated women approaching our Special Cell. After participating in gender awareness programmes, I was able to see socialisation through the gender lense.

I now understand that it is very important to work with men also to prevent violence against women, Because, in the patriarchal structure of society, men are squeezed and are unable to express their emotions. When I see my journey in the Special Cell, I realise how I have moved away from masculinity to humanity.

—Lakshmikant Kamalajkar

Social Worker at Special Cell from 2003 to 2010

Voice 2

गेली सहा वर्ष मी "महिला व मुलांकरिता सहाय्य कक्ष" मध्ये समाजकार्यकर्ती म्हणून कार्यरत आहे. सदर कक्षामध्ये काम करीत असताना माझ्या वैयक्तिक दृष्टीकोनात खूप फरक पडला. स्त्रीवादी विचारांची ओळख कक्षात कामाला सुरुवात केल्यावर खऱ्या अर्थाने झाली. मी स्वतः पितृसत्ताक विचारसरणीत वाढलेली असल्यामुळे

अनेकदा सुरुवातीच्या काळात स्वतःशीच एक वैचारिक संघर्ष होत होता. उदाहरणार्थ स्त्री ही स्त्रीची शत्रू असते असे मी ठामपणे म्हणत असे. पण कामाला सुरुवात करण्याआधी आमचे जे प्रशिक्षण झाले तेव्हा माझा या विषयाकडे पाहण्याचा दृष्टीकोन बदलला.

कक्षात नेमणूक होण्याआधीची मुलाखत, गटचर्चा, एक दिवस कक्ष निरीक्षण, पुन्हा मुलाखत, त्यानंतर प्रशिक्षण, हि सर्व प्रक्रिया कामाची ओळख करून देण्यासाठी, स्वतःची काम करण्याची क्षमता व स्वतःचा दृष्टीकोन तपासण्यासाठी तसेच कामासंदर्भातील संवेदनशीलता, गांभीर्य यांची जाणीव करून देण्यासाठी महत्वा ची होती.

कक्षात आल्यावर माझ्यासाठी ज्ञानाचे अनेक दरवाजे उघडे झाले. अत्याचारग्रस्त स्त्रियांबरोबर काम करिताना माझे network तसेच वाचन वाढले. पितृसत्ताक पद्धती स्त्रियांवर होणाऱ्या अत्याचाराला कशी कारणीभूत ठरते याचा अभ्यास करता आला. स्त्रियांसाठी असणाऱ्या कायद्यांचा अर्थ उलगडू लागला. समाजकार्याची नीतिमूल्ये, casework ची तत्वे खऱ्या अर्थाने समजली. केलेले वाचन उपयोगात आणण्याची संधी उपलब्ध असल्यामुळे ज्ञानात वाढ होत गेली. कक्षामध्ये भेटलेल्या प्रत्येक स्त्रीकडून मला खूप शिकायला मिळाले. इतरांना ऐकून घेण्याची जी क्षमता माझ्यामध्ये विकसित झाली त्याची मूळ प्रेरणा कक्षात येणारी स्त्री आहे.

वर्षानुवर्षे चालत आलेल्या पितृसत्ताक पद्धतीने, समाजव्यवस्थेने स्त्रीयांना दुय्यम दर्जा दिला आहे. या विचारसरणीत वाढलेल्या स्त्रीपुरुषांना स्त्री ही एक माणूस आहे, तिला तिचे हक्क, अधिकार असतात हे पटवून देणे खूप कठीण काम आहे. स्त्रीवादी विचारसरणीने कक्षात काम करीत असताना "तुम्ही फक्त स्त्रियांचीच बाजू घेता" असे वाक्य अनेकदा कानावर पडते. तेव्हा स्त्रीवादी विचारांनी काम करणारी कार्यकर्ती ही पुरुषविरोधी नाही पण कोणत्याही परिस्थितीत स्त्रीवर केला जाणारा अत्याचार सहन केला जाणार नाही याची जाणीव करून द्यावी लागते. पोलीस विभागासोबत काम करीत असताना हा विषय संवेदनशीलपणे त्यांना पटवून देणे ही एक अवघड गोष्ट असते. परंतु विषयाचा सखोल अभ्यास असेल व आपण आपले विचार ठामपणे मांडले तर ते प्रभावी ठरते याचा अनुभव अनेकदा

आला आहे.

पोलिस स्टेशन मध्ये काम करताना crisis च्या केसेस बऱ्याच वेळा येतात. धुवांधार पावसात आपल्या सात मुलांसह बेघर केलेली एक महिला उपाशीपोटी एकदा कार्यालय बंद व्हायच्या वेळी कक्षात आली होती. त्यांच्या खाण्यापिण्याची सोय करून, पुष्कळ प्रयत्नानंतर तिच्यासाठी व तिच्या मुलांसाठी आधार गृह शोधून त्यांना तिथे पोचवून मी घरी गेले, तेव्हा मध्यरात्र झाली होती. या केसेस मधून खूप काही शिकावयास मिळते आणि एक प्रकारचा आत्मविश्वासही वाढत जातो. स्त्रियांवरचे अन्याय, अत्याचार पाहिले ऐकले कि काही वेळा खूप तणाव येतो. परंतु अशावेळी सहकाऱ्यांशी चर्चा, विचारविनिमय तसेच विवेकनिष्ठ विचार करण्याची सवय यामुळे हा तणाव दीर्घकाळ राहत नाही. महिला व मुलांकरिता सहाय्य कक्षात काम करणे माझ्यासाठी खूप आत्मिक समाधान देणारे आहे.

I have been working with the Special Cell for Women and Children as a social worker. I liked the process which the Special Cell follows. Before appointing the social worker, there is group discussion, s/he gets to understand the work where the candidate meets the team, sees the work and then both decide if the the worker can work in the Special Cell. The induction training is also very useful.

My perception of violence against women has changed. There are so many times when there is internal conflicts between one's socialisation and the ideology in the Special Cell.

Working in the Special Cell has opened so many doors for me. My network has increased, I read a lot, have understood how patriarchy plays a role in the violence against women. I understand the principles of casework. I now understand the rights of women as those for an individual and not in other prescribed roles. There is no justification to violence. Explaining all this to the violated woman and other stakeholders including the police is not an easy task, it requires a lot of confidence and self-belief.

When you are sitting in the Special Cell at the Police Station, there are crisis cases which you have to handle. There are times when women come in just as you are about to leave the office for the day but you have to support them. Listening to them and handling cases of violence takes its toll, but talking and sharing all that happens with your colleagues and analysing the situation helps in reducing the tension.

Working in the Special Cell is very satisfying for me and I have learnt a lot from the women coming to the Special Cell.

—Rani Date

Social Worker at the Special Cell from 2000 to 2017

Voice 3

My 17-year career started with working on the issue of violence against women and children. The Special Cell for Women and Children, then a project of Tata Institute of Social Sciences, Mumbai, and visionary Prof Meenakshi Apte gave me this tremendous opportunity to work with the Cell and to understand the ambit of violence in our society.

For a person like me who has come from a low socio-economic background, who has always been taught by society and family that women are born for subjugation, to serve the men in their life, and never to raise their voice for their rights and to obey orders–this opportunity was an awakening and was tremendously empowering. I was able to realise my basic rights, which the Indian constitution had granted me from the time when I was in my mother's womb, after 23 years of age.

This work was an eye opener. It helped me understand the police as an organisation, the criminal justice system, women's status and the existence of violence at every step–in–society as well as political lethargy and absence of will towards certain issues. The understanding of the game of power and the systemisation of violence within society fascinated me, and continues to drive me to work with powerful state machinery like the police

The work satisfaction was so great that I don't think I would get it anywhere else. I worked on all issues, from training police personnel from various States, to replication of Special Cells across Maharashtra. The aspects of work involved right from working with individual women to policy makers, to law formation, to the demystification of the Acts in favour of women and children. The work needed a lot of commitment, perseverance and sensitivity. It taught me that life is as beautiful as it is ugly. If each individual respects and is sensitive towards others it is beautiful, but if he/she crosses these lines it is ugly. The work and the women with whom I have worked made me a very strong person, to the extent that no problem remained a problem, and I accepted all challenges as a routine part of life. The work with women and children also made me more and more responsible, and a sensitive human being. When women used to come to meet me as a Cell Worker to discuss their issues, I used to feel and understand the depth of their sorrow before they could even start speaking of their violence. This was the language of hearts, which taught me the meaning of 'sisterhood'.

I experienced sisterhood within the organisation as well. While working on an issue like violence against women, one needs lot of hand-holding, psychological and emotional support. At the Special Cell we colleagues had a strong bond. My colleagues were my support system and were like my extended family. A person like me, who had never stepped into Mumbai prior to my admission at TISS, felt completely safe and secure working in Mumbai, primarily because of my colleagues and the Mumbai Police.

Whatever little power and position I had while working with the police system I used entirely for the oppressed sections of society. I was in Mumbai for ten years, working tirelessly. The work became like addiction. Every day I used to look forward to going to the Cell and talking to women to absorb their worries. The basic objective of the Special Cell was to create a platform for the women to vent. This platform has evolved to be a super model and is now being replicated in the rest of India.

—Ranjana Gaikwad
Social Worker

Voice 4

टाटा सामाजिक विज्ञान संस्थेत च्या दुसऱ्या वर्षी शिकत असताना कार्यानुभवासाठी मला महिला सहाय्य कक्षात काम करण्याची इच्छा होती. त्यासाठी जेव्हा मी अंजली दवे यांना भेटले, तेव्हा त्यांनी माझा पंधरा मिनिटांचा वर्गच घेतला. इथेच कार्यानुभव का घ्यायचा आहे, कामाच्या स्वरुपाची कल्पना आहे का असे बरेच प्रश्न विचारले व मला विचार करायला भाग पडले. आधी इथे काम केलेल्या senior शी चर्चा करून निर्णय घेण्यासही त्यांनी मला सुचविले. विद्यार्थ्यांना कामाची पूर्ण जाणीव देऊन निवड करण्याची संधी देण्याची ही प्रक्रिया मला फारच आवडली. कार्यानुभवासाठी तर मी तिथे गेलेच, पण शिक्षण संपल्यानंतर कार्यकर्ती या नात्याने महिला सहाय्य कक्षात कामासाठी रुजू झाले.

कक्षात काम करू लागल्यावर प्रोबेशन वर असताना कांदिवली, दादर व तसेच पोलिस आयुक्तांच्या कार्यालयात असलेल्या अशा तीनही कक्षांत काम करण्याची संधी मला मिळाली. इतर कार्यकर्त्यांच्या कार्यपद्धतीचे निरीक्षण करून मला माझी पद्धत विकसित करिता आली. प्रत्यक्ष काम करताना अनेक प्रश्न डोक्यात यायचे. पुढे काय करावे ते कधी कधी सुचत नसे. परंतु बरोबरच्या कार्यकर्त्यांशी चर्चा करून मार्ग काढता येई. सर्व कार्यकर्त्यांची दर महिन्याला होणारी बैठक हे तर monthly tonic वाटायचे. यातून बरेच काही शिकायला

मिळत असे, काही चुकले असेल तर त्याचे गांभीर्य व पुढे काय दक्षता घ्यावी ते लक्षात येत असे, कामात येणाऱ्या शंकांचे निरसन होत असे आणि पुन्हा जोमाने काम करायचा हुरूप येत असे.

विद्यार्थी म्हणून सहाय्य कक्षात काम करीत असताना एकदा रात्री एकटीनेच पोलिस ठाण्यात जाऊन एका केस संदर्भात अधिकाऱ्यांशी बोलायचे होते. मनात धडकी भरली होती, पण रोमांचही होता. पोलिस ठाण्यात जाऊन आत्मविश्वासाने अधिकाऱ्यांशी बोलले. अशा अनुभवांनी पोलिसांची भीती तर गेलीच पण पोलीस हे वाईट असतात ही पूर्वकल्पनाही बदलली. सहाय्य कक्षाच्या कामात पुढे जात असताना व्यक्ती म्हणून माझ्यात व माझ्या विचार करण्याच्या पद्धतीत बदल होत होते. एक प्रशिक्षित कार्यकर्ती म्हणून अधिकाधिक स्पष्टता विचारात येत होती आणि ती कामात उतरत होती.

१९९७- ९८ मध्ये सहाय्य कक्षाच्या expansion व institutionalisation साठी महाराष्ट्र सरकार बरोबर चर्चा सुरु झाली. या प्रक्रियेत UNIFEM सारख्या जागतिक संस्थेची व शासनाची महिला प्रश्नांवरील भूमिका समजण्यास मला मदत झाली. याआधी महिला कक्षात मदतीसाठी येणाऱ्या स्त्रियांचे रोजचे प्रश्न मला महत्वाचे वाटत होते. पण आता larger picture पाहिल्यावर policy level वर झगडण्याचे महत्व कळू लागले. सहाय्य कक्षाच्या विस्तारीकरणानंतर नवीन कार्यकर्ते निवडताना त्यांची महिला प्रश्नांसाठी commitment पारखणे ही एक जबाबदारी वाटू लागली. त्यांचे प्रशिक्षण करताना स्वतःच्या कामाचे पुनर्विलोकन व विश्लेषण करता आले.

२००१ च्या strategic management exercise मध्ये मी सहभागी होते. सहाय्य कक्षाचे काम हे विविधांगी आहे. अत्याचारित स्त्री, तिचे कुटुंब, न्याय यंत्रणा, पोलिस यंत्रणा, शासन अशा अनेकविध पातळ्यांवर काम करताना कक्ष कार्यकर्ते सुद्धा अष्टपैलू होतात व एका वेळी विविध व्यवधाने सांभाळायला शिकतात. कक्षाचे हे विविधांगी कार्य यथार्थतेने शासनापुढे मांडण्यासाठी strategic management exercise द्वारा श्रीमती राजश्री मथानी यांनी आम्ही करीत असलेल्या प्रत्येक कामाला स्पष्टता देण्यासाठी मूल्यांकन चाचणीची निदर्शके निर्माण केली. सहाय्य कक्षाच्या कामाचे प्रलेखन, संशोधन व नवीन कार्यकर्त्यांच्या प्रशिक्षणासाठी २००७ मध्ये Resource Centre for Interventions on

Violence Against Women ची स्थापना झाली. आतापर्यंत केलेल्या कामाला शब्दात रुपांतरीत करून इतरांपुढे मांडण्याची कला या साऱ्या प्रक्रियेतून आम्ही शिकत गेलो.

सहाय्य कक्षात केलेल्या कामाच्या अनुभवामुळे कुटुंब न्यायालयात समुपदेशक पदावर माझी निवड झाली. सहाय्य कक्षात काम करिताना कार्यकर्ती म्हणून खूप स्वातंत्र्य होते. आपल्या पद्धतीने हस्तक्षेप करता येत होता. न्याययंत्रणेबरोबर काम करताना नियमांना धरून चालावे लागते. पण महिलांचे प्रश्न तेच, परिस्थिती तीच व समाजही तोच. पोटगी , घटस्फोट, स्त्रीधन, एकत्र नांदणे अशा मागण्या घेऊन महिला सहाय्य कक्षातही येत असत आणि न्यायालयात न जाता कौटुंबिक, सामाजिक पातळीवर त्या सोडविण्याचा आम्ही प्रयत्न करत होतो. कक्षामधील कामाचा पूर्वानुभव असल्यामुळेच कुटुंब न्यायालयात मी समुपदेशन सहज व परिणामकारकरित्या करू शकले, आणि करत आहे.

As a student of the Tata Institute of Social Sciences, from the second year I wanted to work in the Special Cell For Women and Children. I had met Anjali Dave, she explained to me the functioning of the Special Cell and also told me to think it over and come up with 'Why I would like to work with the Special Cell'. I also met the senior social worker in the Cell and discussed my wish to work with the Special Cell with her. I liked the kind of process work they told me about very much. As a student, I had approached the Police Station regarding a case. Interacting with the officers at the Police Station gave me a lot of confidence but I still could not get over the general perception that the police are not good in cases of violence against women.

After my graduation, I joined the Special Cell as a Social Worker and during my probation period, worked in all the three Special Cells at the time–namely Dadar, Kandivali and at the Police Commissioner's office. Working in all the three offices and interacting with the social workers there helped me to develop my own style of working. The monthly team meetings were like a tonic.

In the year 1997-98, during the process of expansion, I understood the larger picture on violence against women, the importance of working at a policy level and the stand international agencies like the UNIFEM took on the issue of violence. I also learned the process of selecting and training new social workers for working in the Special Cells.

The strategic management exercise with Rajshree Mathani, which started in 2001, helped in bringing about a lot of clarity in our work and developed the monitoring indicators. 'The Resource Center For Interventions on Violence Against Women' was started in 2007, which helped in consolidating our work in the field into concepts.

On the basis of my experience in the Special Cells, I was selected as a counsellor to the Family Court. There is a lot of independence in working in the Special Cell but in the Family Court there is a prescribed format, but the women came with the same problems. In the Special Cell we tried helping the women at the pre-litigation stage, this helped me in taking up the role of counsellor easily and doing result-oriented work.

—Vandana Shinde

Social Woker

Voice 5

I joined the Special Cells as a social worker in 2001. There was a Special Cell in Ulhasnagar at that time. I had worked earlier in a Family Counselling Centre and wanted to work with women. When I joined, though I had some experience of dealing with cases of violence against women, I found that the approach of the Special Cell differed from the approach of the Family Counselling Centre in a number of ways. At the Special Cell, the intervention was done with a feminist perspective, there was no insistence on reconciliation and the worker could take many decisions independently, without interference from her superiors. In those days such trust in the capacity of workers was rarely shown in other organisations.

At that time there was no formal induction training of new workers in the Special Cell, as we have at present. However, the current practice of keeping a new worker on probation for three months, during which she spends one month only in observation of the work done at the Cell, and a review at the end of the probation period existed even then. In those days, training was informal, and on the job. We (the Cell social workers) were a small team and we used to constantly inform each other about our work and take each other's advice. We developed strategies for work in consultation with each other. There was a formal meeting once a month with the coordinator, where we used to discuss our work.

The formal induction training of new workers started when the first expansion took place in 2002. The training module currently in use was not developed then, but we used to cover the same topics of VAW, gender, laws and counselling skills. Training was done every time there was an expansion of the programme. On the basis of that cumulative experience, when the expansion in Haryana took place in 2007, the training module that we use now was formalised.

The Ulhasnagar Special Cell received funding from UNFPA, which required us to write periodical reports of our work. Thus began our work of documentation. The intake register was in use to record client information since my date of joining, but the other systems of documentation developed in response to the needs felt on the job. The monthly and quarterly formats for monitoring and evaluation were developed only after the expansion of the programme.

At the time of the first expansion, the Vision Mission Statement and the Monitoring Indicators of the Special Cell were developed. The consultant for the exercise, Rajshree Mahtani used to come to the Ulhasnagar Special Cell and take our inputs to understand the district perspective, as at that time this was the only Special Cell that was functional at a district location. We were all excited about the expansion, but I was concerned that our pro-woman perspective might not be executed with the same fervour by NGOs selected to implement the Special Cells after institutionalisation with the government.

In 2000-2001, as a part of a government drive, many training programmes were initiated for the police, which were also attended by Public Prosecutors and Forensic Officers. The Special Cell was involved in these programmes as a trainer on issues of VAW, gender and child sexual abuse.

We were also invited more than once to conduct training sessions at the Police Training School at Marol. I had organised Police Training at Ulhasnagar. While this was on, we received a message that Akshardham in Gujarat had been attacked and a Red Alert has been sounded. At such a time, the police are supposed to drop everything else and report to their assigned place of duty. But the Deputy Commissioner of Police, acknowledging the importance of the training programme, allowed it to proceed uninterrupted.

When the Protection of Women from Domestic Violence Bill was being drafted, Prof Anjali Dave made a presentation in Parliament, based on the inputs from the Special Cell. Indira Jaisingh held a session with the Special Cell Workers about the Bill, and sought our feedback about whether we saw ourselves as Service Providers or as Protection Officers under the system that would be set up by the legislation.

When UNFPA withdrew its funding in 2006 after the programme became institutionalised with the government,

Thane district was selected over Ulhasnagar to set up a Special Cell during the second phase of expansion, and the Ulhasnagar Cell closed down. I then worked in Dadar for some time. Later, I became the coordinator. The transition was not difficult, and I was happy with the opportunities of growth it offered. But I must acknowledge that casework with women is infinitely more satisfying than administrative work. I clearly recall a case where I facilitated a woman's legal separation from her violent husband and the joy and relief with which she came to thank me. Work with women yields handsome rewards.

Working at the Special Cell has impacted me as a worker and as a person. I learnt to look at a woman as a person; I learnt to look at things more conceptually. I became more confident and learnt to negotiate my own rights sternly and effectively. This work has given me exposure to working with individual cases of women facing violence as well as with the systems.

My vision of the future of the Special Cell includes a more streamlined structure and a better recognition of the work of the Social Workers in the Cell by the government authorities. I hope this service reaches more survivors of violence and that they get the required support at all levels.

—Divya Taneja
Social Worker

A Perspective from the Police

Dr Ravindra Singhal, Commissioner of Police, Nashik

I have had a long association with the Special Cells.

We were instrumental in starting the Nasik Special Cell. I was the Superintendent of Police there at that time.

The Cell workers were very active. They used to discuss many of the issues related to women with the police. I feel that in the process of empowering women, the Special Cell workers as well as our staff also evolved.

In Nanded, for the first time, we gave a special office to the Special Cell in 2007-2009. In case the women came with children, we had made special provisions such as arranging for toys so that they had a homely atmosphere. We provided the Special Cell with a dedicated telephone line, vehicle, staff and stationery. We allotted to the Cell police staff who were properly trained. The police and the Special Cell workers enjoyed a very cordial relationship.

In Nanded, we involved the Special Cell in outreach activities as well. For instance, if we came across news of a woman facing harassment, the Special Cell unit would be given a police vehicle, and the concerned police station would be informed, and they would reach the village of the woman and do the needful intervention. This sent a very good message. Two things happened: first, this created awareness amongst people about the services of the Special Cell, and second, it established goodwill for the Cell. If there was a good case, the newspapers would highlight it. Registration of cases at the Special Cell went up. In some cases, there was reconciliation. If that was not happening, the Cell workers would help the women to file cases under the law. In both situations, the workers were playing a very important role.

In Nagpur, I was Additional Commissioner of Police (Crime). There the Special Cell workers would handle cases of women, but they had started other activities for children in the slums such as their education, guidance, and counselling.

The location of the Special Cell within the police station is very important. Our staff and the Special Cell staff together create a safe space for the victim, or rather, for both the parties. If the Special Cell did not create an atmosphere of security for the opposite party, it would hamper the process. The opposite party might not reply to the questions put forth by the workers. Though the Special Cell staff is wearing plain clothes, the presence of the police and the location being a police station makes a big difference to the psyche of both parties.

I feel that the relations between the Special Cell and the police depend on how well they both cooperate and how the police leadership sets the norms. If the Commissioner of Police gives the Cell workers proper guidance or if the Police Inspector is favourably disposed towards the programme, if they have regular meetings with the Special Cell staff, if they keep checking the data provided by the Cell workers – then this system works well. I have had a good relationship with the Special Cells everywhere.

The Cell workers are quite competent and interested in their job. Whoever I have worked with has been very good. They are eager to learn. They have been very forthcoming–they used to discuss cases with me, they asked me to follow up on the cases–such practices are good and are required.

We used to consult them for some of the issues related to women. In our crime meetings we used to ask them to deliver lectures to our staff. Because of this, they got recognition within our staff and the message went out that these people have the backing of the unit commander. We did this with the aim of helping women and children under threat of violence.

Expansion of the Special Cell is a positive step, because everybody is concerned about women's issues, especially after the Nirbhaya incident. Expansion of Special Cells to Taluk levels is a welcome development, because the mindset of the society needs to change. In order to be able to empathise with the problem of women and girls, the mindset of the police also needs to change. This can happen through the Special Cells.

Exposure to the Special Cell practices and interaction with the workers can help bring a positive change in the system. The Cell workers compile data about their work, which can provide the basis to change plans and laws for the benefit of the woman. There is an increased awareness about violence against women. There is also an increased need to take action. Until and unless we involve society, we will not be able to give justice or may not be able to reach victims of violence.

My vision for the Special Cell is that I would like to see the Special Cells acting in a more pro-active manner. *What is happening right now is that they start intervention when the victim comes to them. What should happen is that these Cells should reach out and intervene in cases of violence that get reported in the newspapers.* They themselves should go and contact the victim in such cases, and get the case registered. In addition to helping that woman, they would be spreading the message that a woman facing violence is not alone; there is help available for her. This way, they would be empowering all women. Hence, I see the role of the Special Cells as a programme with potential to be more pro-active and transparent. Now the police are also better trained, and will be able to give the workers the required support. Together, they can ensure that justice is delivered to women facing the threat of violence.

Feminist Social Work Intervention: Social Workers' Voices

THIS CHAPTER SEEKS to understand the nuances of feminist social work practice based on the experiences of the key stakeholders (i.e. Social Workers) in the Special Cell intervention process. The authors have tried to explore the elements of feminist social work practice and identify the discourses that the social workers use to understand the men involved, their behaviour, the intervention, and the men's response to the intervention.

This chapter engages with social workers, to discuss their experiences with and analysis of feminist social work practice. Social workers were interviewed by the authors and their names have been changed in this book in order to preserve confidentiality. They were asked to reflect on their practices and work at the Cell, as coalescing around the following questions:

- How do Special Cell social workers see their own work in relation to the complexities of VAW?
- What are the approaches/main components of the intervention of Special Cell that social workers think facilitate change for men?
- What motivates social workers to work in the specialised field of VAW response/direct intervention in crises?

Despite variation in approaches, convergences between feminist principles and social work practice have been constant throughout the developments in both fields. Feminist theory has the capacity to play a greater role in enabling social work practice to become more anti-oppressive and inclusive. There are some clear non-negotiables emerging from a convergence approach towards feminist social work practice, which can be described as follows:

- *Belief*: When it comes to interventions and working with survivors as well as perpetrators of violence, social workers work with a belief that all human beings can change – and it is on this premise that further conversations take place, while establishing the non-negotiable understanding that violence against women is a crime.
- *Goal*: The goal of the intervention is to stop violence against women, and violence against the client. The way to achieving this goal in the *joint intervention* and through interventions at the Special Cell, is to challenge the man's violence, hold him accountable for his violence and work towards his commitment to change. The goal is social and political change, not personal or individual adjustment to social conditions.
- *Women-centered practice*: The interventions at the Special Cells use joint work as a means to achieve the goal of alleviating violence from a woman's life. What is

important here to note is that joint work is not neutral. The woman is always at the center of interventions and it is only possible to undertake joint work when current violence has ceased. The aim is to facilitate a process for the woman to become personally empowered to be able to bring about desired change in her own life.

- *Client self-determination*: The self-determination of the woman is paramount in this process. The options range from her wanting to stay with the man who has subjected her to violence to willingly and amicably part ways. The woman must feel safe in both living with her partner and participating in joint intervention before such interventions can proceed, at her request.
- *Responsibility for violence*: It is extremely important for the man who has used violence in the past to take full responsibility for his violence, and not to share blame with the woman. The social workers at the Cell, at the very beginning of the intervention, establish that violence is not a mutual issue and both man and woman should acknowledge that the onus of abuse is on the man. The man must be willing to be accountable for his actions, both past and future and work towards overcoming his violence. He should acknowledge that his behaviour was a choice, not a matter of loss of control.
- *Standpoint of the Special Cell*: When it comes to violence against women perpetrated by other women, the Special Cell takes the position that other women are not the enemies; and that change can be brought about in social relations between women, as well as between men and women. This is why the intervention process includes individuals, joint work, and family work, as and when required and requested by the client, in order to reevaluate

and reassess these relationships in order to develop mutual empathy. This is done to develop respectful behaviours and attitudes to replace abusive ones.

Thus, we see that overarching components connect the various forms of feminist and social work interventions: awareness and acknowledgment of the social and political context in which both the social worker and clients exist, and a firm grounding in feminist philosophy and social work values. It is the integration of these two factors that establishes feminist social work practice as a model for social and individual change.

Feminist social work intervention is a process in which the woman is at the centre of the intervention, in an environment of trust and safety that enables her to explore, understand and manage her own problems. The feminist approach to social work has its root in the understanding that problems faced by clients are not located within the female psyche, but rather within our societal structure, which is patriarchal and oppressive. Therefore, the goal of this perspective is to create a society that is equitable and free of violence.

Feminist social work intervention is a collaborative exchange and process that encourages the client (woman) to participate in the world and engage with her social and political realities. *This type of intervention differs from others because its primary goal is to empower the client (woman).* In a feminist intervention setting, the social worker and client engage as equals and the social worker helps the client realise that not the social worker, but the client herself, holds the source of solutions and has the power to make decisions and take charge of situations. All expectations, roles and responsibilities of both client and social workers must be explored and equally agreed upon at the beginning of the intervention.

Women-centered Social Work Principles

The approach of the Special Cell described above has evolved organically from the work of the social workers located in police stations. The approach of the Special Cell is to work with women to empower them and stand up against violence, and to work with men by challenging them to take responsibility for the violence they commit. As one social worker emphasised, 'When a woman comes to the Special Cell, we don't call her a victim. We call her a survivor, a fighter, who is fighting for her rights because she has already begun her struggle to fight for change in her situation…' (Pooja). The term *victim* acknowledges that the woman is violated and acknowledges the abuse that she is facing, but in the process takes away her agency, and the power to address her situation and make essential choices and decisions towards redressal. The word *survivor* on the other hand, acknowledges her control over her own life and gives her sense of agency and strength, which is a key feminist goal'.

The Special Cell social workers draw on the shared values of feminist perspectives and social work principles – social justice, dignity and the worth of an individual. Feminist ideology identifies that women grow up in a suppressive, patriarchal society and the goal of the feminist social worker is to address the social problem of patriarchy to help the woman/person in need and move towards self-determination and empowerment. The intervention at Special Cell thus focuses on helping them develop strategies for identifying and breaking away from traditionally oppressive and restrictive roles. This is reflected in what Asha has to say, 'When we talk about our approach at Special Cell, we talk about helping the woman and making her strong. We have to work with her to recognise violence and bring her out of her blame. Some women are so well-moulded in patriarchal socialisation that they think violence is normal. We have to help her first focus on empowering herself and helping herself discover how to break the stereotypes and binds of some traditional roles that women play that may be blocking their development and growth'.

While talking to social workers, two of the survivors expressed the paradox of the cultural roots of violence against women, by emphasising a cultural dichotomy where women are either revered as goddesses or treated like chattel. Asha explained the issues of culture and patriarchal control that emerge in their sessions with men, saying, 'We see this traditional mentality all the time in the sessions and we have to constantly challenge this patriarchal mindset. For example, Hindus believe that a trace of the mother is present in every woman. What is the use of this belief and of worshipping Laxmi, Saraswati and Durga when their human representatives are treated like chattels? We live in a society where mothers are often coerced and degraded for giving birth to girls, unborn girls are killed in wombs, daughters-in-law are ill treated and beaten, expectant mothers get beaten during pregnancy....'

Some participants also believed that a woman-centered approach meant working towards the safety and security of women as well as children. Women who are being subjected to domestic violence often have mental health needs. Women experiencing domestic violence report that their children have witnessed or have themselves been beaten during an incident of physical violence. Exposure to domestic violence is now recognised as a form of emotional child abuse, so children in families where a woman experiences violence very often need support too, and need to be moved to a temporary shelter (or to have the violent man leave the home) in order to make it safe. This compound the complex web of needs, which the social worker must untangle.

The task of the social worker is to offer support and information to challenge the woman to examine for herself which road she wants to take, rather than offering didactic advice. This is described by a social worker very succinctly as follows: '...I call myself *streevadi* (feminist) because we work in the Special Cell to empower the woman. We work from the perspective of the woman and what she wants. It is a difficult and a time-consuming process but at the Special Cell, we support the woman to make her own choices. This helps her handle her life better in the long run.'

Feminist interventions at the Special Cells tend to be more focused on strengthening women in areas such as assertiveness, communication, relationships and self esteem. Manisha emphasises, 'The woman needs to be prepared and strengthened to be able to go for a joint meeting. Preparing her to talk, to make her challenge her husband who is violent is never easy for a wife. Preparation is mainly so that she can talk on an equal footing and power balance can be equalised. We need to arm her with tools needed to do that. In our presence that is achievable. The woman has our support and the Special Cell being located in the police station gives her additional power'.

The empowerment approach to work with women in Special Cells is also described by the social worker as challenging and complex. The practice of this approach inherently involves an ongoing tension between the social worker's wish for the client's safety, and the practical realities of the woman's life, with all the ambivalence that typically arises in abusive intimate partnerships. Some of the social workers shared that quite often in the work of domestic violence, a woman will make a choice to return to an abusive partner, initiate contact with a partner against whom she has filed a protection order or criminal cases or make other choices that compromise her safety.

However, the social worker's responsibility, often deeply challenging, is to devise intervention strategies that will ensure the woman's safety within her choices, without dictating or making decisions for her. As Rajanya points out,'We are doing pro-woman work with which the woman should feel empowered. It means a lot of things that are challenging. It means that we help women think through their problems. We believe in the principle of self-determination and we help them make informed choices. This sometimes is a huge dilemma for us as social workers. Sometime a woman who is in a very abusive relationship still makes a choice of reconciliation and in this situation the work of the social worker becomes very crucial – to work with a man in a strategic manner. The *ranneeti* (strategy) as we call it has to be very robust and workable for woman and for the man'.

Thus, working with specific needs, and tailoring interventions in order to make them best-suited to the client is a strategy social workers use to address these challenges.

Khadija, for instance, highlights that very often women expect a certain degree of guidance, and often experience helplessness due to the erosion of their sense of self-worth through violence. She has noted that, 'The woman is her own expert and self-determination is very important for us in Special Cells. It is not an easy process. The woman many a times comes and asks us "Madam what should I do, you tell me?" She wants ready-made solutions but our approach at the Cell is to help her think through her options, reflect on her reality and help her make informed decisions. This is a long and a painstaking journey'.

Rajanya adds to this narrative, 'She may see us social workers as hierarchical figures and expect some direction to deal with immediate stress as well as guidance in understanding her options and reaching her goal. This is also because we are located in the police station. In fact, some women may drop out of Cell intervention if we are perceived as being completely non-directive. Clients also want to learn their options very quickly and learn skills early on so that they can use it in their day-to-day lives'.

Social workers at the Special Cell understand violence against women as a complex social problem, with gender inequality at its core. All the participant social workers have noted that several factors can contribute to the situation of conflict and stress in the intimate life of a couple, and that when handled poorly, may result in violence. At the same time, they hold the view that the men are fully responsible for choosing to act violently when they instead could have acted in other, less harmful ways.

However, social workers interviewed for this study found that sometimes, women are not able to name the violence and recognise it as wrong, due to patriarchal socialisation and the belief that wife beating is connected to masculinity. As Asha points out, 'When a woman comes to the Special Cell, I have observed that many a times violence is not her major issue. Most of these women have either compromised or normalised the violence and have accepted their situation as fate. There are other issues such as the man is not paying children's fees, throwing her out of the house, in-laws isolating her and neglecting her as she is of another caste or religion, non-consummation of marriage, issues of man having "out of marriage relationships". Thus, relationships are complex, and violence is multi-layered'. Working with women thus often involves emphasis in the first instance, on the fact that violence itself is wrong and is a crime.

Social workers largely agree that police intervention is necessary to protect the woman and that without such intervention, the violence escalates. However, they observe that both police involvement, and the criminal justice system response that follows, do not adequately and fully address the needs of both the men who use violence and the women survivors who have approach them for help. Asha says, 'Women approach the police station with a hope that the man who has subjected her to violence will be set straight by the police. When she goes to the police, there is a hesitation from their side as it is a "personal matter" of the family. The police, in this case, come from their own experience of dealing with families where the inter-family dynamics change very frequently. This is where Special Cell comes in. Once the woman comes to the Special Cell, she gets a space to negotiate/or not with her partner'.

Some of the social workers also talked about the diversity in problems, and the profiles of the kind of people who approach the Special Cell. In exploring these issues of diversity as practitioners in Special Cells, we have to consider a growing body of work on the intersectoral and intersectional nature of domestic violence. *Special Cells intersectoral and intersectional work aims at understanding women in relation not only to their experiences of gender inequality, but also the social division of class, race, age and disability.*

This attention to diversity speaks more directly to the experiences of a significant group of women who find themselves 'on the margins' and do not necessarily identify gender oppression as the primary frame through which they understand their lives, even when they live with violence and abuse from their partner or ex-partner. As Rajanya points out, 'Women and men come to the Special Cell from various backgrounds and we as social workers need to understand and handle delicate dynamics of firstly gender, then socio-economic class, inter-caste, inter religious marriages, cultural practices, issues of age, sexual orientation and disabilities'.

Domestic violence can impact the survivors, their families, and their social networks on multiple levels. Special Cell social workers work at all levels, both individual and systemic – with the violated person and the perpetrator, with families and communities, and on the issue of family violence within the public/state system as well. Social work involves structured and multi-faceted interventions, and the network building, advocacy, and wider interventions scope is a part of the commitment of social workers to bringing about sustainable and lasting change. Feminist theory stresses that the 'personal is political' and social work theory emphasises the 'person in environment' – both of these are important perspectives focusing on the client's social location, and specific surrounding environment.

Through these understandings, social workers theorise that that individual woman's experience of isolation, shame and fear can only be addressed through understanding her political, social, economic and cultural context. As Vijay says, 'Men who are violent towards their intimate partners have either learned or discovered that they can use violence to get their way as the woman will keep quite because of shame and stigma and fear of isolation and will not receive support. At Special Cell, we try and help her break this isolation and silence by connecting her with environment for support and help cope better with social functioning'.

At the Special Cell, not only are contextual factors important, but also the process of work. The end is important but the means to the end is also crucial, as described by Vijay: '...Without social work principles and tools and techniques of case work, we can't work effectively in bringing change in men's behaviour. I believe that the basic value of social work, that every human can change, gives us great strength at challenging times when we look at a man who has used extreme violence and force on his partner and think that he will not be able to change. Another principle, which gives me great support while working with men, is a non-judgmental attitude. It helps me keep my biases in check and not judge people as bad, horrible and hopeless.'

Social workers at the Special Cell recognise that engaging with relationships and social networks is often the key to change. The social worker of the Special Cell talks about the significance of helping the client find supportive relationship in their lives, either with the partner, family or any other relationship. Joint and group/family interventions here become a medium or a platform to create these networks and relationships. However, here it is important to note that even if the social worker is intervening with an intimate partner/husband or the family, it is not with a focus on 'preserving' or 'saving' the family; but with a women-centered focus, with the understanding that the woman in an oppressed and subordinated position needs support to be able to voice her concerns and to determine what she wants.

In fact, joint meetings are often encounters for the survivor, where the social workers' main role is to support the woman in voicing her needs and making her feel safe and strong in this encounter. Pooja emphasises, 'Joint meetings are very important but before that, a lot of preparation work needs to be undertaken by us as social workers. Individual meetings with both the parties help us to understand how each one is thinking – what they want, what is achievable etc. Our work is guided by what the woman wants, so preparing her to speak, supporting her to determine for herself, developing her confidence all goes a long way. A lot of ground for what she wants is covered in individual meetings, emotions are handled so that both are more open and anxieties and uncertainties are less – and this preparation really helps in the joint meeting where the woman is able to put forward her pain and challenge his violence and discuss options for the future'.

Feminist and social work principles reflect a broader commitment to reaching and helping women and promoting equitable social relations. Social workers identify this principle as a reason for accepting men's applications at the Cell, as a strategy for reaching and helping a woman who may potentially be facing violence. Vijay explains, 'At the Special Cell, we take men's applications too. We take his application when he approaches the Special Cell saying she has left the home and gone away to her natal home. We look at this as an opportunity to reach out to the woman and mostly, in my experience, I find that when we reach out to the woman, we find her to be a violated woman'.

One of the social workers shared how she created safety and security for the woman through the intervention process, a step which was of prime importance in this case. Very often, even though women desire reconciliation, first ensuring their safety is the key task of the social worker before the option of joint meetings becomes at all viable. This view of the social worker shows the multidimensional work with people, systems and law, and the need to validate women's perspectives and foreground the concern for women's safety. Asha, the social worker in charge of one case, gave us the example of how difficult and complex a case can be.In this case, a 21-year old Muslim man was in love with an 18-year old Buddhist woman, whose parents had passed away. She was therefore living with her aunt and uncle. She discovered that she was three months pregnant, but when she told her partner he panicked, denied paternity, and threatened her and told her not to tell anyone. She thus came to the Special Cell, where her immediate safety was a prime concern as the man's family had become threatening and aggressive. Thus, the social worker made immediate arrangements for the woman to stay in a shelter home.

The police then registered a case of cheating, even though it was a consensual relationship with the promise to marry, to make sure the woman was safe. The man's family was not open to an inter-religious marriage and insulted the woman with caste-based slurs. The Special Cell employed the help of the police to insist that the man come forward and take responsibility, and after interventions they decided to continue the relationship, as the man accepted responsibility for promising to marry her as well as the paternity of the child.

The woman, through counselling, was made aware of her options and that she could chose to terminate the pregnancy – however she wanted marriage, and to stay with her partner and have the baby. Her partner agreed to this, and eventually the family and Quazi (Muslim religious leader) who had been involved in the case, had to agree as well.

Asha, in her intervention, thought that there was an immediate threat to the client's safety in the new environment with a hostile marital family, so after the marriage, she visited her, and created a neighbourhood watch group who would support and connect with the client. The local village representative (Police Patil) was also alerted to the situation and would check to ensure that she was safe.

This case shows that another unique feature of the Special Cell is that the case is never technically closed. Interventions might end, but social workers always tell the woman client that their doors are always open for her whenever she needs help. This is done with an understanding that the overcoming abusiveness is likely to be a lifelong process and keeping the probability of relapse in mind. Vijay stresses that, 'at the Special Cell, no case is ever closed. Women can approach the Special Cell again and again and this gives an important message to both men and women – that the Special Cell and Special Cell social workers are always there to support them. This message helps a lot while engaging with violent men'.

Strategies for Working with Men at the Special Cell

Feminist theory and practice emphasise that men are socialised into violent behaviour, and some feminists have highlighted the need to work with men on addressing and challenging this socialisation. It is interesting that different social workers have emphasised different strategies and technique for the process of bringing about change in these men. Some social workers at the Special Cell believe that challenging the men's socialisation and gender roles is necessary to stop their violence on intimate partners, whereas others say that identifying the need to create a respectful and safe environment is of utmost importance.

Some saw men as desiring power and control and hence thought of working on creating space where the woman and man can talk about power imbalance, and how power can be shared for a more equitable relationship. Some of the social workers have identified a trend – that men minimise, deny and blame their partners for their violence to achieve power and avoid taking responsibility for violence. All the participating social workers agree that listening to the men's experiences of injustice is extremely important, but they also feel that sincere listening has to be followed up with making the man aware and conscious of his reality and use of violence.

Some social workers have suggested caution, adding that listening to the men's experiences of injustice should not be interpreted simply as collusion with the men, in making excuses for their abusive behaviour. Social workers are cautious not to excuse or justify the violence through psychological or social explanations of being oppressed but to see how to confront the man in a way that protects the violated woman's interests.

During the interviews with social workers for this overview, it has become apparent that they have a complex understanding of their work with men who are violent towards women. Vijay has pointed out: Men too come to social workers, initially showing that they are victims and are vulnerable and they are falsely blamed. But once they open up and see that we are there to help them through this, they confess their bad (abusive) behaviour and actually want to change and want family and children and a better life. They realise what a mess they have created.

At first, there is an innate resistance from men at the Special Cell: because of the police location, and because of the emphasis on women, spelled out in the very name of the Special Cell – this emphasis on a space specifically for women makes them assume that it will be biased against them. Asha notes: Men come with all kinds of attitudes and emotions to the Cell. They might be angry and upset. They are sometimes aggressive as well, which is a manifestation of the shame of being called to the Police Station. They blame their wives and say the women have spoilt the family name. At this time, our role as social workers is of utmost importance – we have to deal with them with calmness and respect. It is difficult not to get angry and irritated, but we have to do it in the interest of the woman and from our value system as trained social workers.

Pooja further clarifies this position by stressing that:The Special Cell works with a primary focus on women. This work cannot be done leaving the man behind. It is in the interest of the woman that we need to engage the man constructively. We have to keep what is central – what the woman wants and deal with the man.

Overcoming initial resistance to engage in the intervention requires effort from both social worker and the men. Most men participants, after their first interaction with the social worker, become calmer and more willing to begin the engagement process. The special skills used by the social worker in overcoming initial resistance contribute to making the man feel invited into the space to listen to his story.

'When men come huffing and puffing about why they are called to the police station, we calmly inform them that we are social workers working with the police. We are not the police. I always tell them we are here to listen to you and help you – inviting him to tell me his side of the story. This helps to convert the window shopper into customer, that is – a reluctant client into a client, who will start engaging with the social worker', says Rajanya.

Vijay adds, 'it is a general trend that no man accepts that he was violent. Rather he starts blaming his wife and other family member. But when we start working with them and make them aware about their behaviour and its impact on the woman and children, by way of reality orientation, they do start to accept their mistakes and see their own excuses'.

Here the social workers affirm that the way in which the man is received and treated in the first meeting plays a crucial role in developing the rapport to a more indepth working relationship of trust. Pooja explains that 'they come with a mindset that this is Women's Cell and they will not listen to me. At the end of the first meeting, my objective is to listen to him, let him know that I understand him, make him feel at peace and bring down his defenses and invite him to come again with thoughts about what he thinks about change. In most cases, men are also looking for a platform where issues in their life can be sorted – so Special Cell becomes that bridge between a man and a woman'.

Another part of working with men is supporting them to change and challenge violent behaviour. In many cases, couples go through many cycles of violence, but in some cases, men might be able to change their ways after participating in intervention processes that are designed to re-educate, motivate and engage them in a change process. These narratives of social workers reflect their belief in change, which allows them to employ creative thinking and strategies in engaging with men for that change.

Vijay, a male social worker, says, 'the first and the most important aspect of the intervention is that men have to be encouraged to talk about their life issues and their difficulties in some way or the other. They are also victims of patriarchy. They have to be able to unlearn and relearn the socialisation which has taught them to be violent and oppressive'. However, Asha cautions that 'if the social worker plays supportive role besides confrontation, men do start the process of change – but it's not easy for them to change in this environment of male dominance and privileges they enjoy being a man'.

All social workers working in the Special Cells have stressed on women's concern as the central focus of intervention, and the need to engage with men with discernment, respect and clarity of purpose so that the interest of the violated woman is protected and the man can start acknowledging violence and develop commitment to change.

Another social worker has explained the significance of listening to men's perspectives through a focus on women, stating that, 'Women are the focus of our work at the Special Cell. The men with whom we work feel that they are not our primary "clients" as they know that they are coming to the Special Cell "for women". We constantly state that we do this work for the protection of women and children. Working with men is a means whereby we can achieve this end of protecting women and children. Mind you, this by no means imply that they are treated disrespectfully, or that they are unimportant to us. In fact, in my experience, if we treat men badly and blame and shame them, we lose them. In Special Cell, we find that men appreciate the openness with which they are treated. Listening to the men's perspective help us support the woman better and not put her in any danger'.

A male social worker at the Special Cell explains that in a patriarchal society, there are not many formal and informal agencies that help in facilitating democratic discussions. The Police, Panchayats and elders of the family, are all entrenched in patriarchal gender norms and are often highly didactic. Thus, when a man is heard openly, it helps him build rapport with the social worker and reduce resistance. As Vijay said, 'Listening helps the man gauge the worker's sincerity... if you really listen to them in a dignified, non-judgmental way and with respect, they get the message that the worker really cares for them. This creates an environment and rapport to challenge/confront men's violence on women and give a clear message that it is a crime'.

However, Asha has a different approach. She says, 'In my experience, I feel that men easily understand the language of power. Because of Special Cell and its pro-women focus, men get the message that now women have their own space and power in the police system'. Rajanya extends this approach, by arguing, 'The man tends to see that he has to lose something and he fears this. Most men are brought up with having their way in our patriarchal culture. They think if they lose, the wife will have her way, the society will look down upon them. To suppress the wife's voice, men use power, position, possessions, persona. So, with men, we have to focus on shared interests and not on individual positions: what is to be gained or lost?' Thus, she uses a strategic approach in her interventions with men, with a focus not on 'who wins', but developing shared goals for both parties.

Pooja advocates a balanced and intersectional feminist approach: The main aspect I keep in mind while working with the man is his background, his community, his class, his educational background. This gives me a window into the belief system and thinking process he might be coming with. I am not talking about being biased or making a judgment, but trying to understand where he is coming from so that I can reach out to him better and make better assessment which can benefit women and facilitate the process of work.

Hierarchy and power is embedded in the location of the Special Cell. The social worker has to do the delicate and sensitive work of engaging the men in the process of change in self, as well as relational change, and at the same time remind him of the possibility of legal action if he continues to violate the rights and dignity of the woman survivor. Vijay shares his strategy of work in this respect: Helping men recognise their resistance, anger, harming behaviour ... simply attacking or confronting someone directly does not always work – it may drive people deeper into their shell or lead them to be highly defensive. Encouraging the man and boosting his confidence that he can change and working with him to identify the area of change, is helpful. Men start with the victim position. It's only much later that they realise their power and privileges. We have to do emotion-focused work which will help him address the woman's and family safety and dignity, which is the core of Special Cells work.

Writing assurance papers are one strategy of working with men, to concretise decisions and promises that emerge from the intervention. Assurance papers are written by the perpetrators (not by clients), where assurances to end violence and commit to positive behaviours decided on during the intervention, are listed and signed by the perpetrator, and accepted by the client. The social workers felt that this is a powerful tool to create a written record of the man's committment to non-violence and other changes.

This document also creates a sense of security and safety for the woman though it is not always that a man is willing to pen down his change. Rajanya summarises: Writing an assurance paper is another way to get the man to commit to whatever he says in writing. This system of assurance paper emerged when the woman involved said that if he wants me back in his house ask him to give it to me in writing that he will not beat me. *This over the years has become a regular and a powerful strategy* we use for the woman to have a proof of his commitment to non-violence.

The key informants were very clear on their ideology and approach, that there could be no blaming the wife, excuse or justification for violence. As one social worker succinctly summarises: We help individual women to determine what she wants, and if she wants nonviolent reconciliation then we strategise so as to stop the violence first and then to strengthen the relationship of the couple. The couple have to be able to a) see the problem from the other's point of view; b) identify key issues and concerns such as violence, blame and use of power by the man; c) determine what shared outcome would be acceptable (or good) for both men and women, and then d) look for new ways to achieve these by changing current patterns of interaction which are violent and controlling of the woman. In this process the key message is that violence is not acceptable and man cannot negotiate that.

It is important to recognise that social work interventions with men are always characterised by dynamism, contradictions and contestations. It is on the basis of this dynamism that a social worker plans and strategises interventions and challenges resistance, while intervening with men, working toward gender justice and progressive pro-feminist masculinities.

Motivations and Challenges in Work on Violence Against Women

Choosing to practice social work in response to violence against women in particular, is not an easy decision. However, social workers in their interviews cited a range of positive effects and implications for this work on their own lives, including the sense of making a contribution, of the satisfaction of doing work that is congruent with one's values and beliefs, and of receiving client feedback to strengthen their belief in the work. We have known social workers who have withdrawn from VAW/domestic violence work because of the troubling effects it had on them emotionally. Others have withdrawn because they have lost belief in the efficacy of their efforts or have simply got burnt out.

The narratives speak of emotional effects, sometimes loss of hope, and of the danger in the work involved; and how, through this, conviction is sustained. Asha explains, 'Many a times, we take the burden of the women's cases home. The work is so emotionally intense that a controlled emotional involvement is not always possible. There are times when women decide to go back to their violent relationships not recognising dangers of the situations, and we as facilitators feel responsibility for their safety'.

As a feminist social worker, especially women who come from a shared history of oppression, there is a strong feeling of sisterhood which social workers share with women clients. Social workers also shared the value they found in the work, their pride in the interventions, and their own contributions to social justice. Vijay emphasises: My belief in feminist ideology makes me a pro-feminist man. It is important to state my position when I am doing work on violence against women. As a man, I have a lot of responsibility to engage with men and women to take the message of gender equality to people.

The Way Forward

In conclusion, we at the Special Cell have to say, the feminist social work framework is a participatory and equitable framework, which brings together values and principles that take us closer to a more just and equitable society. Patriarchal values are deeply embedded in our society, and the social workers at the Special Cells thus need to integrate feminist perspective in their practices in order to understand and address the cultural context as well as the needs of the client.

To counter women's oppression, subordination and violence, it is important for the social workers to have gender aware perspectives and take a strong feminist, woman-centred stand. Social workers of the Special Cell have provided their insights on a spectrum of intervention work and processes – such as a client's right to self-determination, a social worker's duty to protect the safety of the client, reporting of domestic abuse to the police, good practices for addressing domestic violence, practicing with cultural competency and an intersectional orientation – and navigating the complex terrains of joint interventions with the clear goal of ending violence against women. Their insights and challenges provide fertile grounds for developing and nuancing understandings of feminist social work praxis at the Special Cell.

Roadmap for Growth, and a Vision for the Future

The Special Cell has seen tremendous growth since its inception – both in scale and breath of services provided, as well as in the evolution and depth of its critical feminist social work praxis. This document, through its engagement with clients, social workers as well as the police, has attempted to capture the more recent decades of the work of the Special Cell, and the insights the work at the Cell offers for feminist social work interventions with the state.

This chapter ties together key threads across this book, and briefly presents recommendations, and a vision for the future of the Special Cell and continued multi-agency interventions work.

'A Felt Need': The Enduring Necessity of Multi-Agency Response to VAW

The Special Cell, as discussed in an earlier chapter, was described by the police in the early 2000s as a 'felt need'; a deeply relevant intervention which brought value to the police as well as the community of survivors. A decade later, the Special Cell remains relevant, as evidenced by the growing demand for services; as well as data on violence and perpetrators. Not only is the magnitude of violence against women far from abating; the need for systemic partnership and engagement is as crucial as it was in the 1980s.

The data collated from the ten years post-expansion in Maharashtra shows that the 13 Special Cells reviewed undertook in-depth process-oriented work with 17,962 registered clients, and engaged in 27,955 one-time interventions (where persons with specific queries received complete assistance within one meeting itself). This vast number of newly-registered clients nearly doubled, from an average of 117.3 persons per Cell per year in 2003, to 203.6 persons in 2012. There was also an increase in the average number of one-time interventions (regarding referral, information, guidance or crisis) per Cell from 136.4 in the year 2003 to 343.1 in 2012.

The increase in the average number of new-registered clients as well as persons seeking one-time interventions reflects both, *the need for such services* as well as the acceptance the Special Cells have earned within the police system and the community. The referrals data is also telling, in the high percentage of referrals from ex-clients and the police (38% and 26% respectively in this review). The large numbers of women who have been referred by ex-clients signify high client satisfaction with the service, as well as the engagement of the Special Cell with the police system.

Another factor obvious by comparing data across the decades of the inception of the Special Cell, is evidence that violence perpetrated by men, and marital families, remains a pressing concern, which requires strong systemic response – the state must intervene and deliver women's rights. Overwhelmingly and consistently, perpetrators of violence are the husbands of clients, and women clients continue to primarily be of the reproductive age group, 25-34 years (42%). The family is thus not a safe space for women, but is often a site of violence and oppression, and it is crucial for feminist interventions to bring familial violence to the notice of the state.

The idea that violence within families is private, and is insulated from the ambit of the state's responsibility, must be continually challenged, and one strategy for such challenge is partnership with state systems in order to direct resources and police commitment towards underserved communities. Whereas it is possible that perceptions that the Special Cell deals primarily with domestic violence may have set in, entailing greater representation from this group of women, it is undeniable that women in marriages continue to face severe and multiple forms of violence, and are increasingly turning to institutions such as the police for support in ending this violence. Clients require a spectrum of supportive services – both institutional support and strong backing and affirmation from state systems to affect an end to violence; as well as safe spaces within systems where their voices will be heard and valued.

Data from the Special Cells also reveals the magnitude of diffused impact of violence on women's lives and provides evidence that violence does not only manifest in physical abuse but takes many forms. In recognising and recording multiple forms of violence and their interconnections, it becomes evident that while mental and physical violence by the husband are the most reported forms of violence (57% and 61% respectively), financial violence and dispossession from the marital home (38% and 17%) are also significant, along with sexual violence (15%, which may be underreported due to stigma associated with revealing these details), when one considers the magnitude implied by entire range of clients over this decade.

It becomes clear also from the data on past help sought, that women do not turn to the police and state systems as a knee-jerk, first response, but continue to struggle and find means of intervention from social and familial networks. As Special Cells records show, 43% of women first turned to their parents for help, and many turned to other sources like panchayats, friends and acquaintances, and hospitals and referral centres. This not only reflects the fact that women proactively seek an end to violence and turn to formal state institutions as a last resort, but also the diversity in the kinds of help and intervention they require.

The success and growth service like the Special Cell, which provides support to women throughout the process of accessing support from multiple systems and services (and not only referrals), presents *evidence for the need for increasing and strengthening a convergence approach to interventions and promoting multi-agency response, with a focus on state support and accountability.*

Empowerment and Autonomy Towards Rights and Change

Above all, the Special Cell works towards the empowerment and autonomy of women survivors and recognises how patriarchal social systems are at the root of violence against women. Thus, the broader mandate of the Cell is to work through a feminist, rights-based approach towards dismantling patriarchal systems of oppression and effecting wider social change.

Client narratives identified specific benefits of the intersection of feminist intervention practice and state support. One of the benefits identified was women's increased ability to navigate systems, and to confidently demand their rights from the police. Inculcating an understanding of, and determination to access rights, is one of the key tenants of the Special Cell; and clients over the years have been able to take steps – some small, some bigger, towards independence and assertion of their right to a life without violence.

Confidence-building was a major thread in client narratives. As Saroj narrated, when she had to navigate the family court, she felt very depressed. However, the social worker became a source of moral support during this time. She said, 'I came from a very rigid family, where words like court and police are unthinkable and inaccessible, to women as well as men'.

Although ideas like divorce had previously been alien to her, she was able to confidently navigate the family court. She said,'Now I am confidently handling all situations. If I talked about myself, the word "fear" is no longer in my dictionary. My confidence has increased, my body language has changed, I have increased my friend circle. Housewives always feel hesitant to talk to men, but now I don't feel hesitation'.

Neena adds, in her narrative, the importance of harnessing the authority of the state to advocate for women, through feminist praxis. She said that it was only through the intervention of the Special Cell that her husband became amenable to the idea of intervention and reform. She said, 'I went to the police station to make a complaint against husband. They suggested that there is no point in making a complaint, as this means only punishment. The said, you go to the Special Cell, if you feel comfortable, then take counselling, it will be better for you. So, on the second day I went to the Special Cell. The social worker explained that she will listen to both parties, and at the Cell they do not take complaints: whatever the decision will be, you both will have to take yourselves. When the social worker called my husband, he avoided the call. But then the social worker insisted that if he didn't come, she would have to take police help. Then he became serious and came to the special cell along with me... If I had not come to the special cell, my husband's behaviour would be the same as earlier – he would still be doing the same thing. But after coming to the cell, he changed. Today I am very much satisfied; I feel free. According to me, the violence is zero now. Now even if my husband tells me to separate, then I am ready to do that. My self-confidence has increased'.

Social workers narrate that even small changes they observe in their clients are indicative of seismic shifts in their sense of self. Even observing a client taking more care with her appearance, looking happier and well-turned out, are indicative of a shift towards self-care and confidence – a crucial indicator of change for women survivors. Neha said that after intervention from the Special Cell, she now works, has a job, and supports herself. This brings her peace, and she has a dream to go abroad, and is applying for a passport.

The social workers, in their testimonies, also narrated the impact their work at the Special Cell had on their own understandings of empowerment and change. As Ranjana noted: For a person like me who has come from a low socio-economic background, who has always been taught by society and family that women are born for subjugation, to serve the men in their life, and never to raise their voice for their rights and to obey orders – this opportunity was an awakening and was tremendously empowering. I was able to realise my basic rights, which the Indian constitution had granted me from the time when I was in my mother's womb, after 23 years of age.... The work and the women with whom I have worked made me a very strong person, to the extent that no problem remained a problem, and I accepted all challenges as a routine part of life.

The empowerment work of the Special Cell is thus an ongoing and diffused process, rather than a finite goal or objective – spread across stakeholders, clients and interventionists. As Divya said, 'Working at the Special Cell has impacted me as a worker and as a person. I learnt to look at a woman as a person; I learnt to look at things more conceptually. I became more confident and learnt to negotiate my own rights sternly and effectively'.

Social workers also described increased independence and autonomy in working at the Special Cells as empowering; as well as the creation of a network of interventionists and support. The Special Cell also works to build networks across services, NGOs, activists and women; and in this network, clients and stakeholders alike draw support and commitment towards shared goals of ending violence against women. Divya said, 'At the Special Cell, the intervention was done with a feminist perspective, there was no insistence on reconciliation and the worker could take many decisions independently... In those days such trust in the capacity of workers was rarely shown in other organisations'. Ranjana adds, 'I experienced sisterhood within the organisation as well. While working on an issue like violence against women, one needs lot of hand-holding, psychological and emotional support. At the Special Cell we colleagues had a strong bond. My colleagues were my support system and were like my extended family'.

Working with Systems

The Special Cell's close work with the police system continues to be a crucial and unique model in VAW redressal services. Working with the state and creating a model for effective police-based social services; in its three decades of experience in the Maharashtra context, the Special Cell has become an important example and proof that such state-based services are valued by women and are necessary in widening and strengthening the nets of support available to them.

As a police official has astutely pointed out: The location of the Special Cell within the police station is very important. Our staff and the Special Cell staff together create a safe space for the victim, or rather, for both the parties... Though the Special Cell staff is wearing plain clothes, the presence of the police and the location being a police station makes a big difference to the psyche of both parties... I feel that the relations between the Special Cell and the police depend on how well they both cooperate and how the police leadership sets the norms. If the Commissioner of Police gives the Cell workers proper guidance or if the Police Inspector is favourably disposed towards the programme, if they have regular meetings with the Special Cell staff, *if they keep checking the data provided by the Cell workers* – then this system works well.

The Special Cell's thriving within the police system rests on support from the system, as well as close and constant engagement with the police personnel on a daily basis. At the Cell, the police and social workers are colleagues, with differing expertise and methods, and both must work towards the goal of ending VAW. The presence of the police and location within the police system is thus not only strategic in harnessing police support for the survivor, but also in demonstrating to perpetrators that women have the support of the state, and that domestic violence is not private or a prerogative, but a crime.

It is important to note that 39% women report that they had previously sought assistance from the police before coming to the Special Cells. This underlines the fact that while these women do require support from police and the state, the support provided to them was not effective in ending violence. This points towards the need for continued advocacy and training of police personnel, and closer work with the police in order to improve the delivery of services from the police directly. It is also likely that police personnel who are posted in proximity to the Special Cells are more aware of the work of the Special Cell and are able to refer clients to the Special Cell; yet referral must also go hand-in-hand with effective police support for survivors. Additionally, within the police system personnel are subject to transfer. Thus, new personnel also require orientation, as do new inductees into the police force. It is clear that advocacy with the police force should be system-wide and ongoing. *Referrals from the police helpline also remain low*; presenting another area for further advocacy.

An important part of the work done by social workers is also facilitating women in seeking justice from formal justice systems and courts. The Protection of Women from Domestic Violence Act (2006) as well as Section 498A of the Indian Penal Code are two important legal provisions specifically for women survivors of domestic violence; and the social workers as well as the police have an important role to play in ensuring women are able to seek justice under these provisions.

Section 498A in particular is a criminal provision, and the police has a crucial role in this regard in investigating and ensuring that the case reaches the court system. Social workers thus work with police, and support women survivors through procedures and the challenging experience of seeing a case through. The enactment of the PWDVA by Parliament in 2006 opened up new avenues for redressal for women survivors of domestic violence, and the social workers at the Special Cells have taken advantage of this new law to help clients seek redressal. The PWDVA presents remedies for women who require multiple forms of support, including financial compensation, restoration of right to shared household, and protection orders – with provision for interim and ex parte orders for immediate relief. However, there is need for stronger implementation, and greater clarity from the State government on the role of Special Cell personnel as Protection Officers and Service Providers, as well as more clarity on the role of the police under the Act (given its civil nature).

Need for a Supporting Helpline Service

The data show a very high number of women coming to the Special Cells for on-the-spot guidance. Though some of them are in a state of crisis and require intense intervention in that single interaction, many have queries regarding location or procedures of the Special Cell, or of other agencies such as shelters or hostels. This points towards the need for a supportive helpline service that is accessible to all women and provides suitable information and referral to individuals who require it. This service will improve the reach of the Special Cell as well as reduce, to some degree, the number of one-time interventions, leaving social workers more time for the in-depth work required with other clients.

As much as 72% of clients are women aged 18 to 34 years, with 42% comprising the sub-group 25 to 34 years. This is where the most visible increase has occurred over the ten-year period covered in this study. By contrast, the number of clients under 18 who use the services of the Cells is low. It is possible that these persons are using other systems established for them, such as the Child Welfare Committee. However, this could be an area for future growth. One strategy could be to strengthen ties with collateral organisations that serve children in various capacities. Social workers at the Cells report that often police personnel recognise their expertise in sensitive counselling and case management and call them in for difficult cases. It is important to expand this awareness across the board.

The calculation of average numbers of clients per Cell may also, in the future, lead to further exploration of what constitutes a manageable workload for social workers. While the scale-up of services has meant reaching out to newer areas, increased client load also places increased pressure on the existing workforce of social workers. It is certainly possible to build the motivation of social workers and to increase their efficiency, but it is equally necessary to recognise that the numbers in the reports cover the intense and demanding nature of such social casework. State authorities should recognise that some centers may be high-volume centers and should ensure that all the planned 144 Cells are established with a clear rationale for the location of new Cells. *The next phase of expansion should also consider evidence-based criteria for increasing the personnel placed within a working Special Cell.*

The Special Cell for Women and Children lives up to its name – 87% of its clientele is women. However, interestingly, the number of men who seek services at the Cells has also increased over the ten-year period. Some of them (5%), as fathers and brothers, approach the Special Cell on behalf of the violated woman but there are also cases of men who bring 'complaints' against women to the Special Cell (7%). When social workers delve further into the case, they often find that the 'complaint' actually stems from the husband's jealousy or from the resistance that women have put up against harassment that originally came from the man in question.

Social workers report that, at least in some instances, men anticipating a formal complaint filed against them by their partners, register a complaint on advice from lawyers. Thus, it is important not to relax advocacy efforts with legal entities over women's rights; while engaging with such cases and providing supportive services to the women facing violence or harassment.

It is important to acknowledge that despite the rich data yielded, the monthly and quarterly reports have their limitations. Given the nature of the data (compiled reports of the Special Cells) we were only able to generate a composite profile of the clientèle. It was not possible at the level of this study to disaggregate information of male and female clients of the Special Cells and to match this information to the interventions provided or their age. Such an exercise would only be possible with the digitisation of records and resources for the purchase of computers, and the use of appropriate software to generate client-wise tracking.

Digitisation of records will increase efficiency, could lessen the burden of documentation faced by social workers, enable detailed analysis of clients and trends, and improve the programme managers' understanding of who is using the Special Cell and develop and nuance intervention strategies. Computerised documentation also make retrieval of information easier, as well as the handling of the extensive volumes of client data generated at the Special Cells. The Gujarat government has already made such arrangements for its Special Cells.

While the most frequently reported problem at the Special Cells is domestic violence, either by the woman's husband or his family, there are also other observable trends with regard to other forms of violence against women: There were 482 cases involving violence due to property disputes and 56 cases of violence in a live-in relationship. Further, though the number of such cases was relatively low, there have also been instances of cyber crime. Trends such as these indicate the need to ensure training of the Cell social workers that is up-to-date, and that they are equipped to handle cases requiring specialised knowledge. Moreover, it is important for the Special Cells to create societal awareness around such issues so that women who are struggling with these problems learn that they have recourse to help within the system, and so that police and representatives of the legal system become aware of the damaging effects of such problems.

The Special Cells for Women approach has offered vast learnings to TISS over the course of adaptation in varied regional contexts. Based on this rich and diverse experience garnered in Maharashtra, the RCI-VAW has begun to experiment with new forms of multi-agency work, and has worked to develop protocols and response structures for the 181 Helpline for women in Gujarat based on the core principles and non-negotiables of the Special Cells for Women approach. Working on new and innovate multi-agency response models for VAW interventions, and further extending work with the criminal justice system, holds the future for such services.

Dr Ravindra Singhal (IG Police, Maharashtra at the time of writing this book), in his vision for the Special Cell, stresses the need for more proactive engagement, and says that it is crucial for the social worker and the police to conduct outreach work to deliver the message that 'a woman facing violence is not alone; there is help available for her' from the system and the Special Cell.

He goes on to emphasise a vision of partnership and facilitation between the police and the social workers of the Special Cells, saying that, 'Now the police are also better trained, and would be able to give the workers the required support. Together, they can ensure that justice is delivered to women facing the threat of violence'. The vision of partnership between state and civil society represented especially by the police and women's movements, for the delivery of justice to women survivors of violence, is central to the mission and ethos of the Special Cell. Women have a right to violence free lives, and it is incumbent on the state to protect this right. Additionally, the police's responsibility is to serve and protect citizens, and advocacy must ensure that this service extends to the marginalised. Innovating with new forms and convergence models for multi-agency work is the need of the hour in the contemporary context of domestic violence.

Special Cells for Women across States of India as on 23.07.2018

At present, through RCI-VAW, the Tata Institute of Social Sciences, Mumbai implements 35 Cells (in 29 districts/ 8 States), and coordinates work of 86 Cells in all (incl. 35 directly-implemented Cells) across 6 States (Maharashtra, Meghalaya, Bihar, Assam, Punjab, Madhya Pradesh, Odisha & Tamil Nadu) & Union Territory of Delhi. Thus, there are 329 Special Cells for Women operational in India (14 States + 1 UT) at present. The following table provides detailed information of the Special Cells for Women operating across the country at present, including those implemented directly by the Institute, as on 23.07.2018:

Type	State	Programme management arrangements	No. of Special Cells
	Maharashtra	Named as 'Special Cells for Women & Children'; Grants-in-aid programme of State Government (Monitoring Committee: Departments of Home, WCD & Police, all funds from DWCD) implemented through franchise model, viz. NGOs appointing social workers, TISS employing 28 social workers & 4 Coordinators (for monitoring, supervision & training)	144 sanctioned as proposed, 124 on paper, 123 functioning on-ground (14 implemented by Institute, 40 directly coordinated by Institute), including at district HQ and taluka-level

Institutionalised (directly implemented by Government)	Gujarat	Named 'Police-based Support Centre for Women'; Entirely funded & implemented by DWCD, through State Gender Resource Centre (1 State Programme Coordinator+ 3 regional Coordinators dedicated full-time to the programme); TISS demonstrated pilot Cells with NGOs (Oxfam India supported) & advocated for institutionalisation (2009-13) and provided technical support to State in establishment & expansion of programme, training & review from 2013-15	**37** (incl. at district HQ & block level) and in process of expansion, as per GRC (State Govt.) website
	Rajasthan	Named 'Mahila Suraksha-evam-Salah Kendra'; Implemented by DWCD (Directorate of Women Empowerment) through grants to NGOs (TISS supported women's groups in pilot demonstration & advocacy for institutionalisation during 2001-2008; thereafter provided technical support to State in training, establishment of programme, review up to 2015)	**41** (in all districts), as per DWCD/ DWE website data

...continued on next page

Special Cells for Women across States of India as on 23.07.2018

	Haryana	Named 'Special Cells for Women & Children'; Directly implemented by DWCD (Coordinating unit within Department incl. Consultant, DEO) with district Police administrations; TISS had demonstrated & advocated for institutionalisation of pilots in 2007-08 with UNDP support, then provided technical support for systems-setting, expansion, training, monitoring & review, research & documentation during 2008-2014.	21 (at the district Mahila Thana in each district HQ)
	Delhi	Named as 'Social Service Units'; Since 2009, TISS has provided technical support (establishment, expansion, training, coordination, review & research) in CAW Cell-based SSUs (now 15) as supported by NCW (funding under Violence Free Home project) and implemented by Delhi Police; 20 SSUs (60 social workers) established in regular Police offices (in February 2018) with MHA funding, direct implementation by Delhi Police and technical support by TISS (RCI-VAW), JMI (Dept Of Social Work) & DU (DSSW/FSW)	15 (Coordinated by Institute, located in SPUWACH.Q. + each of 13 district CAW Cells) + 20 (in divisional/sub-divisional police offices)

Institutionalised (directly implemented by Government)	Uttar Pradesh	Named as 'Crisis-Intervention Centres' under Sakhi One Stop Centre cum Maharani Laxmibai Asha Jyoti Kendra programme, 17 at present directly implemented by Directorate of Women Empowerment (DWCD) with UNICEF support (UNICEF Consultant coordinating Jan 2016-Dec 2017); TISS' tech. support initially.	**17** Sakhi One Stop Centre cum Asha Jyoti Kendra at district HQ since December 2017, as per DWCD information
	Bihar	Named 'Mahila Vishesh Koshang/Special Cells for Women'; State Government Women Development Corporation directly implements 23 in Patna district since 2013 with DFID & UNICEF support; TISS implements 5 pilot Cells (1 each in districts of Gaya, E. Champaran (Motihari), Darbhanga, Bhagalpur & Kishanganj) since mid-2016 with NCW support	**28** (23 Mahila Vishesh Koshang implemented by State WDC with UNICEF & DFID support since 2013 in Patna district, and 5 directly implemented by TISS since 2016)
	Meghalaya	Named 'Special Cell for Women & Children'; TISS directly implements with NCW support	**1** (in Shillong)

...continued on next page

Special Cells for Women across States of India as on 23.07.2018

Pilot units directly implemented by TISS	Assam	Named 'Special Cells for Women'; TISS directly implements with NCW support	**1** (in Guwahati)
	Madhya Pradesh		**5** (1 each in Sagar, Bhopal, Indore, Jabalpur & Gwalior district HQ)
	Punjab		**3** (1 each in SAS Nagar (Mohali), Ludhiana & Amritsar districts)
	Tamil Nadu		**4** (1 each in Greater Chennai, Salem City, Madurai City & Thirunelveli City)
Units operated by civil society agencies with miscellaneous support	Odisha	Named 'Women Support Centres' – 5 pilots established by NGOs with TISS tech. support in 2008-09, continuing Oxfam India funding for 4; TISS established 2 pilot Special Cells for Women in 2018 (Rourkela & Balasore districts) for direct implementation with NCW support	**6** (4 operated by women's groups & NGOs, since 2009 + 2 directly implemented by TISS); 5 more to be established by Oxfam India with NGOs
	AP & Telangana	5 pilots established by NGOs with TISS tech. support in 2008-09, 4 + 2 new continue to be operated by NGOs incl. women's groups like Bhumika Women's Collective, SWARD	**7** (in Hyderabad, Secunderabad, & other districts)

Annexure 1

1

mss

IN THE HIGH COURT OF JUDICATURE AT BOMBAY

APPELLATE SIDE

CRIMINAL APPEAL NO. 359 OF 2008

SOU. RATNABAI JAISING PATIL .. .. APPELLANT

Vs.

THE STATE OF MAHARASHTRA .. .. RESPONDENT

Ms. Mahrukh Adenwala for applicant

Mr S.R. Borulkar, PP.

CORAM: SMT. RANJANA DESAI &

R. G. KETKAR, JJ.

DATED: 10/7/2009

P. C.

On 5/5/08, the Division Bench of this court (F.I. Rebello & K.U. Chandiwal, JJ.) took note of the fact that cases of bride burning and other offences against women are on the rise in the State. The court observed that unfortunately the State has not taken any pro-active steps to sensitise the people in the matter of bride burning deaths. The court observed that pro-active steps in the field of sensitization including the youth in schools and colleges is the need as a long term measure and in short term there is a need to activate the N.G.Os working in the field so as to attempt to bring down the number of deaths. The court further observed that if the State takes pro-active and effective steps it would be possible to eradicate or minimize cases of bride burning and other forms of cruelty to women. A direction was given to the Secretary, Home Department as also Secretary I/c Woman and Child Development Department, Government of Maharashtra, Mantralaya, Mumbai to file an affidavit as to what steps they have taken to discourage bride burning and other cases of offences against women. Necessary affidavit has been filed pursuant to the direction. The court had called for statistics of the cases filed in the Sessions Courts in the State of Maharashtra under Section 498-A and Section 302 of the IPC or other cases of crime against the women year-wise, category wise from 2000 to 2007. We are informed that the said statistics has been forwarded to this court.

2. The Protection of Women from Domestic Violence Act, 2005 ("also referred to as "the Act") is an important step taken by the State to provide for more effective protection of the rights of women guaranteed under the Constitution, who are victims of violence of any kind occurring within the family and for matters connected therewith or incidental thereto. If the Act

3

is effectively implemented it would, in our opinion, eradicate or at any rate bring down the rate of offences against women. Experience shows that as of today there is no effective implementation of the Act because of absence of full time protection officers and service providers at district levels and taluka levels. Undoubtedly the State has made some efforts towards implementation of the Act. Prior to coming into force of the Act, the Government of Maharashtra had issued Government Resolution (G.R.) dated 16/8/01. This G.R. states that Government of Maharashtra is taking over as pilot project the ten counselling centres (Special Cell for Women and Children) which are being run by Tata Institute of Social Sciences since 1984. After coming into force of the Act by G. R. dated 5/12/05 the Government of Maharashtra took over funding of the cells. By further G.R. Dated 17/10/06 the Government of Maharashtra extended the counselling centres to 10 more Districts.

3. The real difficulty, however, arises because of non-availability of full time Protection Officers. We are informed that this work is entrusted as of today to Tahsildars and District Women and Child Development Officers and others. We note that twenty Counselling Centres (Special Cell for Women and Children) have been established and located within the police stations at the district level in 17 (seventeen) districts of Maharashtra under

several Government Resolutions, more particularly Government Resolutions dated 16th August, 2001, 5th December, 2005 and 17th October, 2006. In our opinion, it is necessary to have full time protection officers at the district level and gradually at the taluka level. For the present, in our opinion, the following directions would serve the purpose.

A) One of the social workers that have earlier been appointed in each of the 20 (twenty) Counselling Centres (Special Cell) for Women and Children shall be notified by the Government of Maharashtra as a Protection Officer under the Protection of Women for Domestic Violence Act, 2005, and the other such social worker shall be registered as Service Provider under the said Act within 4 (four) weeks of the passing of this order.

B) The Government of Maharashtra shall establish at the district level in every district of Maharashtra within the jurisdiction of each Police Headquarter, a Counselling Centre (Special Cell) for Women and Children as per the provisions contained in the aforementioned Government Resolutions within 12 (twelve) weeks of the passing of this order.

5

C) One of the social workers to be appointed in each of the Counselling Centres (Special Cell) for Women and Children to be established under clause (B) above, shall be notified by the Government of Maharashtra as a Protection Officer under the Protection of Women from Domestic Violence Act, 2005 and the other such social worker shall be registered as Service Provider under the said Act within 8 (eight) weeks of their appointment.

D) The Home Department, Government of Maharashtra and the Superintendent or Commissioner of Police, as the case may be, shall for its smooth functioning provide for each of the Counselling Centres (Special Cell) for Women and Children the following;

i) an independent room for the Special Cell with some space as waiting area for clients;

ii) postal help to reach call letters to clients, and access to wireless and control rooms;

iii) furniture, i.e., 2 tables, 6 – 8 chairs, 1 cupboard, 2 benches;

iv) stationery;

v) parallel or independent telephone line;

vi) a vehicle from M.T. Section as and when required for

home visits;

vii) an Identity Card / authority letter to the social workers attached to the unit, so that they can visit the police station, access records, jails, lock-ups without any difficulty;

viii) / make available or depute at least one police personnel to help / support the social worker for administration.

E) . The State Government shall appoint full-time Protection Officers at all levels, including the taluka levels, under the Protection of Women from Domestic Violence Act 2005 as prescribed under rule 3 of the Protection of Women from Domestic Violence Rules 2006 by creating a cadre of Protection Officers for the State of Maharashtra as far as possible within two years.

F) The Steering Committee constituted by Government Resolution No. MSK / 2005 / 202 No. 2 dated 21st January, 2006 issued by the Women and Child Development Department, Government of Maharashtra shall monitor and make recommendations to ensure the comprehensive implementation of the Protection of Women from Domestic Violence Act, 2005, including:

(a) making decisions on principles governing the said Act

7

and its execution;

(b) advising on financial management for the implementation of the said Act;

(c) reviewing the programme plans / work plans of the organizing and implementing agencies under the said Act;

(d) facilitating coordination with different arms of the government and stakeholders for the smooth and effective implementation of the said Act;

(e) periodic monitoring of implementation of the said Act by reporting from its functionaries;

(f) developing a criterion for selecting functionaries, such as Protection Officers and Service Providers, under the said Act;

(G) The Judicial Officer's Training Institute for the State of Maharashtra is directed to introduce in its curriculum topics related to violence against women. The assistance of TATA Institute of Social Sciences and the College of Social Work – Nirmala Niketan should be taken for formulating and conducting of such part of the curriculum.

H) (H) The Police Training Academy for the State of Maharashtra is directed to introduce in its curriculum topics related to violence

8

against women. The assistance of TATA Institute of Social Sciences and the College of Social Work – Nirmala Niketan should be taken for formulating and conducting of such part of the curriculum.

(I) The Government of Maharashtra shall create more Counselling Centres (Special Cell) for Women and Children at the taluka level in a phased manner;

5. We hope and trust that the above directions are abided by the concerned authorities so that women get the protection contemplated under the Act and the purpose of the Act is achieved.

(Smt. Ranjana Desai, J.)

(R. G. Ketkar, J.)

Annexure 2

Total no. of Applications	
Year	No. of Registered cases
1984 Jul-Dec	88
1985 Jan-Dec	325
1986 Jan-Dec	315
1987 Jan-Dec	415
1988 Jan-Dec	508
1989 Jan-Dec	407
1990 Jan-June	276
1990 July - Decmber	158
1991 January - Decmber	348
1992 January - Decmber	364
1993 January - Decmber	389
1994 January - Decmber	411
1995 January - Decmber	483
1996 January - Decmber	531
1997 January - Decmber	239
Missing	7
2002 Jan - Dec	600
2003 Jan - Dec	1173
2004 Jan - Dec	1249
2005 Jan - Dec	1324
2006 Jan - Dec	1525
2007 Jan - Dec	1691
2008 Jan - Dec	1929
2009 Jan - Dec	2053
2010 Jan - Dec	2070

2011 Jan - Dec	2301
2012 Jan - Dec	2647
2013 Jan - Dec	4281
2014 Jan - Dec	4421
2015 Jan - Dec	3766
2016 Jan - Dec	3731
2017 Jan - Dec	3987
Total	44012

Annexure 3

Addresses of Special Cells in Maharashtra Implemented By TISS

Location of Special Cell	Address
Police Commissioner's office, Mumbai	Police Commissioner's office, Room no. 36, A Block, Police Quarter Colony, near Social Service Branch
Dadar, Mumbai	Dadar Police Station, Bhavani Shankar Rd, Shaitan Chawki, Dadar W. Mumbai 400028
Kandivali W, Mumbai	Kandivali Police Station, Swami Vivekanand Rd. Opp Shatabdi Hospital, Kandivali W. Mumbai 400067
Vikroli, Mumbai	Vikroli Police Station, Kannamvar Nagar no. 2, Vikroli E. Mumbai 400083
Kurla, Mumbai	Kurla Police Station, Near Bhabha Hospital, Sarveshwar Marg, Mumbai 400070
CBD Belapur, Navi Mumbai	CBD Belapur Police Station, Sector-1, Opp CBD Belapur Bus Depot, Navi Mumbai 400614
Vakola, Mumbai	Vakola Police Station, Nehru nagar Rd., Vakola E., Mumbai 400055
Gangapur, Nasik	Gangapur Police Station., Anandwali–Gangapur Rd., Nasik 422013
Chavan Nagar, Pune	SP Office, Pune (Rural), Chavan Nagar, Pashan Rd., Pune 411008
Wardha	SP Office, Wardha
Yavatmal	SP Office, Yavatmal
Aurangabad	SP Office, Aurangabad (Rural) Near HUDCO T.V. Center, Aurangabad 431003
Vazirabad, Nanded	SP Office, Local Crime Branch, Vazirabad, Nanded
Dhule	Shahar Police Station. Near Bus stand, Shivtirth Rd., Dhule 424001

Annexure 4

महिला व बालकांवर होणाऱ्या अत्याचारास प्रतिबंध करण्यासाठी महिला समुपदेशन केंद्रे स्थापन करणेबाबत.

महाराष्ट्र शासन
महिला व बाल विकास विभाग
शासन निर्णय क्रमांक : मसके-२००६/ प्र.क्र. २५६/ का-२
नवीन प्रशासन भवन, ३ रा मजला
मंत्रालय, मुंबई- ४०० ०३२.
दिनांक : १७ ऑक्टोबर , २००६.

वाचा :- १) महिला व बाल विकास विभाग, शासन निर्णय क्र.संकीर्ण-२००१/प्रक्र.६८/का.२, दि.१६ ऑगस्ट,२००१.
२) महिला व बाल विकास विभाग, शासन निर्णय क्र.संकीर्ण-२००४/प्रक्र.१९/का.२, दि.५ डिसेंबर, २००५
३) महिला व बाल विकास विभाग, शासन निर्णय क्र.मसके-२००५/प्रक्र.२०२/का.२, दि.२१ जानेवारी, २००६

प्रस्तावना :- महिलांवर व बालकांवर होणाऱ्या अत्याचारांना प्रतिबंध करुन त्यांना संरक्षण /मदत उपलब्ध करुन देण्याचे दृष्टीने केंद्र शासनाने प्रामुख्याने ज्या सूचना केलेल्या होत्या, त्या अनुषंगाने उपाययोजना करण्यासाठी अपर मुख्य सचिव (गृह) यांच्या अध्यक्षतेखाली कृतिदलाची (TASK FORCE) स्थापना करण्यात आलेली होती. सदर कृतिदलाच्या बैठकीमध्ये झालेल्या विचार विनिमयानुसार टाटा सामाजिक विज्ञान संस्था, मुंबई या संस्थेकडून मुंबईतील तीन पोलीस ठाण्यांच्या आवारामध्ये सन १९९४ पासून चालविण्यात येणाऱ्या कौटुंबिक हिंसाग्रस्त व पीडीत महिलांसाठीच्या समुपदेशन केंद्राच्या धर्तीवरच आणखी काही ठिकाणी महिला समुपदेशन केंद्रे चालविण्याची शिफारस कृतिदलाने केली होती. त्या अनुषंगाने संयुक्त राष्ट्र संघटनेच्या युनिफेम (Unifem- United Nations Development Fund for Women) या आंतरराष्ट्रीय संस्थेने तीन वर्षांच्या कालावधीकरीता उपलब्ध करुन दिलेल्या निधीतून राज्यात वरील ३ समुपदेशन केंद्रासह एकुण १० ठिकाणी महिला समुपदेशन केंद्रे चालविण्यात येत आहेत. राज्य शासन, टाटा सामाजिक विज्ञान संस्था आणि युनिफेम यांच्यामध्ये झालेल्या सामंजस्य करारानुसार, कराराचा कालावधी संपल्यानंतर सदरील केंद्रांचा आढावा घेऊन उपयुक्त वाटल्यास राज्य शासनाने ती पुढील कालावधीकरीता चालवावीत, तसेच, भविष्यात निर्माण करावयाच्या इतर केंद्रांना देखील त्याच अटींवर मंजुरी देण्यात यावी, असा निर्णय संदर्भाधीन दि.१६.८.२००१ च्या शासन निर्णयान्वये

Samupdeshiy kendra

४. यावरील होणारा खर्च " मागणी क्रमांक एक्स-१,२२३५, सामाजिक सुरक्षा व कल्याण, ०२, समाजकल्याण, १०३, महिला कल्याण, पंचवार्षिक योजनेंतर्गत योजना, राज्य योजनांतर्गत योजना, (२१) (०१) महिला समुपदेशन केंद्रे, (२२३५ ३१७ ७) ४१ सहायक अनुदान," या उपलेखाशिर्षामध्ये सन २००६-०७ या वित्तीय वर्षामध्ये उपलब्ध असलेल्या तरतुदीतून भागविण्यात यावा.

महाराष्ट्राचे राज्यपाल यांच्या आदेशानुसार व नांवाने.

(श. पा. वारे)
उप सचिव, महाराष्ट्र शासन

प्रति,
अपर मुख्य सचिव, वित्त विभाग, मंत्रालय, मुंबई.
अपर मुख्य सचिव (गृह), गृह विभाग, मंत्रालय, मुंबई.
सचिव, (व्यय)/(लेखा व कोषागारे) वित्त विभाग, मंत्रालय, मुंबई.
महालेखापाल, महाराष्ट्र १ (लेखा व अनुज्ञेयता /लेखा परिक्षा), मुंबई.
महालेखापाल, महाराष्ट्र २ (लेखा व अनुज्ञेयता /लेखा परिक्षा), नागपूर
अधिदान व लेखा अधिकारी, मुंबई
निवासी लेखा परिक्षा अधिकारी, मुंबई.
आयुक्त, महिला व बाल विकास आयुक्तालय, महाराष्ट्र राज्य, पुणे.
पोलीस आयुक्त, मुंबई/पोलीस उप आयुक्त (अंमलबजावणी), मुंबई.
पोलीस उपमहानिरीक्षक (महिला अत्याचार प्रतिबंध विभाग), पोलीस मुख्यालय, मुंबई.
मा.मंत्री, महिला व बाल विकास यांचे खाजगी सचिव, मंत्रालय, मुंबई.
मा. राज्यमंत्री, महिला व बाल विकास यांचे खाजगी सचिव, मंत्रालय, मुंबई.
टाटा सामाजिक विज्ञान संस्था, देवनार, मुंबई.
इंटरनेट कॉम्प्यूटर एज्युकेशन सेंटर, धुळे
आधार बहुउदेशीय संस्था, जळगाव
सामाजिक आर्थिक विकास संस्था,पालम परभणी
भगिनी निवेदिता प्रतिष्ठान, सांगली
युवा रुरल असोसिएशन, नागपूर संचलित आपदग्रस्त महिला सल्ला व मार्गदर्शन केंद्र, भंडारा
स्त्री मुक्ती संघटना, दादर, मुंबई
स्त्री मुक्ती संघटना, दादर, मुंबई
भारतीय स्त्री शक्ती, नागपूर
भारतीय स्त्री शक्ती, ठाणे
भारतीय स्त्री शक्ती, अमरावती
संबंधित जिल्हा कोषागार अधिकारी,
सर्व मंत्रालयीन विभाग.
सर्व उपसचिव /अवर सचिव /कक्ष अधिकारी, महिला व बाल विकास विभाग, मंत्रालय, मुंबई.
निवड नस्ती, का.२,

Samupdeshiy kendra

Annexure A

Guidelines for Operating Councelling Centres (Special Cell) for Women and Children

The Special Cells for Women and Children is joint Programme of the Dept of WCD, Home-Police and the Civil Society Organisation/Women's Organisations, located within the Maharashtra police system to work on the issue of Violence against Women and Children. The Special Cell undertakes its work within the Indian Constitution, and work towards ensuring that women are recognised as individuals, with equal rights and opportunities in society, including the opportunity to live peaceful violence-free life.

The Special Cell is esp. located within the police system, to work with a clear understanding that Violence against Women is a crime, against both her and society, and that it is the responsibility of the state to prevent, protect and counter it.

Role and Responsibility of the Steering Committee:

- Policy Development Decisions on Principles and Implementation.
- Advising on financial management of Special cell.
- Review the program plans/work plans of the organising and implementing agencies
- Facilitate coordination with different arms of the Govt and stakeholders for the smooth and effective functioning of the Special Cells
- Periodic monitoring of implementation of the program through reporting from the three partners of the program/ coordinators of the Special Cells
- Develop and plan newer and contextual strategies to deal with Violence against Women.
- Develop a criterion to choose Organising agencies for establishing Special Cells.
- Develop a system for monitoring and evaluation of the Special Cell and organising agencies.

Role of Nodal Department (WCD)

- Be member of the Steering Committee to guide the work of Special Cell
- Provide funding through organising agencies for Special Cell's managed by them.
- Policy Support for effective interventions for implementing agencies.
- Monitoring of the project through periodic visits and reports from implementing agency/Coordinators of the Special Cells.
- Implement evaluation and monitory system developed by the Steering Committee.

Role of DIG (PAW)

- Facilitate and coordinate ongoing day-to-day work of Special Cell to facilitate the setting up of social services within the police system.
- Monitor and supervise guide the Special Cells based on the objectives and Monitoring Indicators of the Special Cells
- Facilitate and coordinate capacity building of Special Cells on socio-legal work with violated women.
- DIG (PAW) will periodically visit the district where the Cells are functioning to facilitate and monitor there functioning to discuss the same with the Co-ordinator and to give feedback to the steering committee
- Be member of the steering committee to guide the work of Special Cell

Role of SP/Commissioner where Special Cell is located

- Support Policy implementation of the program at District level
- Monitoring the work of the Special Cells
- Support/initiate Special Cell District specific interventions on VAW

For the Special Cell to smoothly functioning of the Special Cell, within the police system administrative and infrastructural support is necessary from concerned police unit where Special Cell is located i.e.

- An independent room for Special Cell with some space as waiting area for clients.
- Postal help to reach call letters to clients. Wireless and control room access.
- Furniture- 2 Tables, 6-8 Chairs, 1 Cupboard, 2 Benches.
- Stationary
- Parallel or independent telephone line.
- Providing a vehicle from M.T. Section as and when required for home-visits.
- Providing an Identity card/Authority letter to the Social Workers attached to your unit. So that they can visit police station, access records, jails, lock up without any difficulty.
- Make available/depute at least one police personnel to help/support the social worker for administration

Role of the Organising Agency-

- Implement the program based on the principles and objectives defined for Special Cells
- Appoint suitable trained Social Workers for the intervention
- Orient and train social workers for the work on Violence against Women.
- Day to day Supervision of the program
- Facilitate co-ordination between different stakeholders of the program
- Facilitate on-going training and capacity building of the worker
- Maintain documentation, reports and records of the work.

- Confidentiality of work with violated women must be maintained.
- Financial and administrative decision making for smooth functioning of the Special Cells.
- Submit assessment reports to DWCD and the assessment report format approved by the Steering Committee.

Role of the TISS

- Share the resources build from experience, research and documentation of being an initial implementing agency –
- Facilitation and support planning and setting up of new Special Cells
- Advice and Assist stakeholders of Special Cells on issues of Violence against Women.
- Training and capacity building of different stakeholders
- Participate in Policy Direction/Decisions for the Sp Cells.
- Jointly work on research and documentation with implementing agencies, and other stakeholders of Sp Cells

The Special Cell's approach to work on Violence against Women.

The Special Cell's priority of work is the violated woman, and it is committed to work in the interests of violated woman as a marginalized and vulnerable group. The Special Cell works with all women, irrespective of caste, class, and ethnicity. The Special Cell recognises the violated woman as a person with rights and entitlements, and enables her to gain access to these though the problem-solving process. The Special Cell believes that the violated woman has innate strengths, as well as the potential capacity to make her own decisions, and determine the course of her own life. She is empowered though the problem-solving process, which validates her experiences. The Special Cell acknowledges with humility the violated woman's spirit to survive, and her struggles.

The objectives of the Special Cells are defined as

1. Rebuilding violated women's self-esteem, self-worth and dignity.
2. Offer immediate services in cases of family violence and atrocities against women in the form of:
    a) Police assistance in registering criminal complaints and in any other matter.
    b) Placement in institutions.
    c) Counselling.
    d) Referral to family service agencies and other services including medical, psychiatric, educational and vocational.
    e) Legal aid.
3. Be a liaison between police and organisations for women and children
4. Create awareness among women themselves, among professional groups and general public of the atrocities committed against women and children.

3

5. Document the work of the Special Cell and develop training material for social work students and police personnel.

   The Special Cell's interventions related to the issue of violence against women draws from the framework of Social Work practice and the pro-woman perspective. Further, the role of the Special Cell's social worker is central to the approach of work.

Monitoring Indicators (Operating Procedures or Protocols)

The monitoring indicators have been developed under ten categories, with each category representing an area of work of the Special Cells. Each of these areas is further segmented into specific indicators representing social work interventions within a particular area of work. These indicators are to be used holistically and not individually, as each of them represents a part of the work done at the Special Cells. Monitoring Indicators were developed and finalized in the course of UNIFEM project and are detailed out in book ' Mission Statement and Monitoring Indicators for Special Cell for Women and Children' (2004)

A. Social work interventions for providing emotional support and strengthening the psychological self of the violated woman
B. Social work interventions for negotiating for non-violence with various stakeholders.
C. Social work interventions for building support systems for violated women.
D. Social work interventions for engaging police help in the interest of violated women.
E. Legal Aid to facilitate the violated woman's journey through the criminal justice system.
F. Social work interventions related to arranging shelter for violated women.
G. Social work interventions related to working with men in the interest of violated women.
H. Social work interventions related to the re-establishment of women's relationships with their economic assets.
I. Social work interventions for advocacy for group entitlement in the interest of violated women.
J. Social work interventions related to development counselling with violated women.

Annexure 5

Reporting Formats for Special Cells Mumbai

1. Monthly Report Format, Special Cell for Women and Children

Sr. No	Details	Total
1	New registered cases	
2	Ongoing cases	
3	One-time interaction	
4	Home visits and other collateral visits	
5	Individual meetings	
6	Group meetings and sessions (joint meetings)	
7	Engaging police help	
8	Participation in workshops/conferences/ programmes/seminars/ meetings	
9	Special Cell training-related activities	
a)	Programmes organised	
b)	Resource persons for workshop	
10	PWDV Act 2005	
a)	Referred by us	
b)	Referred to us	
c)	Case registered as P.O.	
11)	Helpline-related activities	
a)	Helpline calls	
b)	Helpline cases	

2. Quarterly Report Format, Special Cell for Women and Children (For 14 Special Cells included in present study)

Sr. No.	Client Profile	Details	Numbers
1	Total clients with whom there was interaction		
1.1	Number of new clients (in this quarter)	Clients who have been registered in this quarter	
1.2	On-going clients	Clients with whom intervention is on-going from the previous quarters	
1.3	One-time interventions in this quarter	Total number of people (apart from clients) who approached the Special Cell for guidance / information / referral / telephone inquiry only once.	
1.4	Total clients in this quarter	New + ongoing + one-time interventions	
2	Clients referred by	Ex-clients	
		Self (client)	
		Relatives	
		Women's organisations	
		Children's organisations	
		Educational organisations	
		Voluntary organisations	
		Jaat panchayats	
		Political party affiliated bodies or political leaders	
		Police	

		Employers	
		Media	
		Lawyers/legal organisations	
		Medical or Para-medical organisations	
		Courts (family court or civil court)	
		Any other (please specify)	
3	Gender of the complainants/ clients	Adults (female)	
		Adults (male)	
		Children (female)	
		Children (male)	
		Any other	
4	Age of the clients	Less than 14 years	
		15 – 17 years	
		18 – 24 years	
		25 – 34 years	
		35 – 44 years	
		45 – 54 years	
		Above 55 years	
5	Education of the clients	Illiterate	
		Functional literacy	
		Primary level	
		Upton matric & HSC	
		Technical/Vocational	
		Training/Semi-skilled	
		Education/Certificate course	
		Graduation	

		Post Graduation/Higher studies	
		Religious education	
		Professional education	
		Any other vocational skills	
		Any other (please specify)	
6	Reasons for registering at the Special Cell (multiple criteria)	Physical violence by husband	
		Physical violence by matrimonial family (other than husband)	
		Emotional/mental violence by husband	
		Emotional/mental violence by matrimonial family	
		Out of marriage relationship/ second marriage by husband	
		Sexual violence in marriage	
		Harassment of natal family members of the woman by the husband/family	
		Deprivation of matrimonial residence	
		Child-battering (by husband/ family)	
		Dowry demands	
		Financial harassment/stress (husband is unemployed/does not report for work/does not give money/harassment over property)	
		Alcohol abuse by husband	

		Substance abuse by husband	
		Desertion by husband	
		Refusal to give maintenance/ streedhan	
		Child custody disputes	
		Deprivation of right to meet children after separation	
		Attempt to commit suicide by client	
		Sexual violence in other situations (molestation/ harassment)	
		Rape	
		Physical violence from natal family	
		Mental harassment at work	
		Physical violence at work	
		Sexual violence at work	
		Unwed pregnancy	
		Child molestation and sexual abuse	
		Wife has left the matrimonial home (male clients)	
		Any other (please specify)	
7	Previous interventions before coming to the Special Cell	Parents/relatives	
		Police	
		Court	
		Women's organisations	

		Other NGOs/activists	
		Any other (please specify)	
8	Types of intervention from the Special Cell (multiple criteria)	Negotiations to stop the violence (woman within matrimonial home)	
		Negotiations for non-violent reconciliation (woman outside matrimonial home)	
		Negotiations to stop the violence in other situations	
		Negotiations for separation	
		Negotiations for divorce	
		Negotiations for child custody	
		Building support system	
		Enlisting police help or intervention	
		Legal aid	
		Providing emotional support and strengthening psychological self	
		Developmental counselling	
		Advocacy for financial entitlements	
		Referral for providing shelter	
		Any other (please specify)	
9	Further referrals by the Special Cell	Medical	
		Psychiatric	
		Police	

		Court	
		Shelters	
		Women's groups/NGOs/activists	
		Relatives/friends of client	
		Any other (please specify)	
10	Other interventions with the community in this quarter	Home visits	
		Visits to institutions (hospitals/ shelter homes etc)	
		Community education programmes	
		Meetings with local groups/social organisations etc)	
		Interactions with police/ bureaucrats	
		Any other (please specify)	

Annexure 6

Documents and Publications of the Special Cell and Resource Centre for Interventions on Violence Against Women

- Panchal T & Shaikh N (1997). *Documentation of police cases of sexually abused girls in Mumbai city between 1994-95.* Tata Institute of Social Sciences.
- Special Cell for Women and Children. (1999). Shades of Courage: Women & Indian Penal Code, Section 498A Mumbai, Akshara Publications.
- Special Cell for Women and Children. (2001). *Because the personal is political: A documentation of the work of the Special Cell for Women and Children (1984-1994).* Mumbai: Tata Institute of Social Sciences.
- Dave A & Solanki G (2001). *Journey from violence to crime: A study of domestic violence in the city of Mumbai.* Mumbai: Department of Family and Child Welfare, Tata Institute of Social Sciences.
- Fernandez B & Gomathy NB (2003). *The nature of violence faced by lesbian women in India.* Mumbai, Research Centre on Violence Against Women, Tata Institute of Social Sciences.
- Meena Deval for Special Cell for Women and Children. (2003). *Mi Majhich.* Mumbai: Akshara Publications (Marathi).
- Apte V (2004). Evaluation study of Special Cell for Women and Children within the Maharashtra State Police System (Jan-Dec 2003). Mumbai: Tata Institute of Social Sciences.
- Special Cell for Women and Children. (2004). *Mission Statement and the Monitoring Indicators for Special Cell for Women and Children.* Mumbai: Tata Institute of Social Sciences.
- Ganesh IM (2006). *Documenting effective interventions and strategic alliances between Maharashtra Police and Tata Institute of Social Sciences.* Mumbai, India: Centre for Equity for Women, Children and Families, Tata Institute of Social Sciences.

- Ganesh IM (2008). *Next steps: Taking the Special Cell process ahead.* Mumbai, India: Special Cell for Women and Children, Tata Institute of Social Sciences.
- Dave A & Pradhan Y (2014). *Assurance Papers: A strategy of the Special Cell.* Mumbai: Resource Centre for Interventions on Violence Against Women, TISS.
- The Special Cell for Women and Children & Resource Centre for Interventions on Violence Against Women (2014). *The Special Cells for Women and Children: Spirit and strategies to meet the challenges.* Tata Institute of Social Sciences, Mumbai.
- Panchal T & Ajgaonkar V (2015). *Let them fly: A multi-agency response to child marriages in Haryana.* DWCD Govt of Haryana & Tata Institute of Social Sciences.
- Dave A, Pradhan Y & Sriraman T (2015). *Changing forms of violence: Violence within non- cohabiting, non-marital relationships- A study of the experiences of intervention at the Special Cells in Mumbai.*
- Resource Centre for Interventions on Violence Against Women. (2015). *A report on cases filed as closed under Section 498A, closed as false in two districts and two cities of Rajasthan.* Mumbai: Tata Institute of Social Sciences.
- Sriraman T (2016). *Paving new pathways: The Special Cell for Women and Children in Haryana (2008-14).* DWCD Govt of Haryana & Tata Institute of Social Sciences.

Bibliography

Special Cells' Perspective on Violence Against Women

- Kennedy, Leslie W in Foreword to *Dangerous Domains: Violence Against Women in Canada* by Holly Johnson, Scarborough, Ontario: International Thomas Publishing, (1996).
- Heise L, Ellsberg M, and Gottemoeller M (1999), Ending violence against women. Population Reports Series L (11) Baltimore, Johns Hopkins University School of Public Health, Population Information Program, December.
- United Nations General Assembly (1993) Declaration on the Elimination of Violence Against Women. A/RES/487104, 1994.
- Mission Statement and the Monitoring Indicators for Special Cell for Women and Children: A Programme for reducing the Violence against Women Within the State Police System compiled by Rajshree P Mahtani and Trupti Panchal (2004).
- Executive Summary Report of 'Strategy Planning for the Special Cells for Women and Children: an Action Research Project (2002–2005)' by Rajshree P Mahtani (2006).

The Way Forward

- Agnes F (2015). 'Section 498A, Marital Rape and Adverse Propaganda'. *Economic and Political Weekly*, 1(23), 1215.
- Apte V (2004). *A draft report of the evaluation study of the Special Cell for Women and Children within the Maharashtra State police system.* Mumbai, India: Special Cell for Women and Children, Tata Institute of Social Sciences.
- Awasthy R (2013). 'Negotiating with Community-based Groups and Structures from a Feminist Perspective' in *Feminist Counselling and Domestic Violence in India* ed. P Bhate-Deosthali, S Rege, P Prakash. Routledge.
- Bombay High Court Criminal appeal no. 359 of 2008. 10/7/2009.
- Bombay High Court Kramank – Mu. Ma. Aa./46384/ appeal Kramank 5647/02; KraMuMa.Aa./ Nondani Kramank 2682/ 11/ Appeal Kra 857/2012/02.
- Bhate-Deosthali, S Rege, P Prakash ed. (2013). *Feminist Counselling and Domestic Violence in India*. Routledge.
- Bhate-Deosthali, P (2013). 'Evolving Guidelines for Running a Crisis Counselling Centre' in *Feminist Counselling and Domestic Violence in India* ed P Bhate-Deosthali, S Rege, P Prakash. Routledge.
- Burte, Aruna (2013). 'The Spirit of Resistance' in *Feminist Counselling and Domestic Violence in India* ed P Bhate-Deosthali, S Rege, P Prakash. Routledge.
- Cunningham A, PG Jaffe, L Baker, I Dick, S Malla, N Mazaheri and S Poisson (1998). 'Theory derived explanations of male violence against female partners: literature update and related implications for treatment and evaluation'. Ontario: London Family Court Clinic.
- Dasgupta, SD (1999). 'Just Like Men? A Critical View of Violence by Women' in *Coordinating Community Responses to Domestic Violence: Lessons from Duluth and beyond* MF & Pence, EL (Eds). Sage Publications.

- Dave A, Y Pradhan and T Sriraman. (2016) 'Changing forms of violence: Struggles in non-marital intimate relationships–A study of the experiences of intervention at the Special Cells in Mumbai'. *Working Paper.*
- Dave A (2015). 'Strategic alliance, a way forward for violence against women: A case for the Special Cells, India'. *Violence against Women, 19* (10), 1203-1223.
- Dave A (2013). *Women survivors of violence: Genesis and growth of a state support system.* Delhi: Orient Blackswan.
- Dave A & Solanki G (2001). *Journey from violence to crime: a study of domestic violence in the city of Mumbai.* Mumbai, India: Department of Family and Child Welfare, Tata Institute of Social Sciences.
- Dunford, FW (2000). 'The San Diego Navy experiment: An assessment of interventions for men who assault their wives.' *Journal of Consulting and Clinical Psychology*, 68, 468 – 476.
- Edleson JL and Eisikovits ZC eds (1996). *Future interventions with battered women and their families: Visions for policy, practice and research.* Thousand Oaks, CA: Sage.
- Ganesh IM (2008). *Next steps: Taking the Special Cell process ahead.* Mumbai, India: Special Cell for Women and Children, Tata Institute of Social Sciences.
- Ganesh IM (2006). *Documenting effective interventions and strategic alliances between Maharashtra Police and Tata Institute of Social Sciences.* Mumbai, India: Centre for Equity for Women, Children and Families, Tata Institute of Social Sciences.
- Gangoli G & Rew M (2011). 'Mothers-in-law against daughters-in-law: Domestic violence and legal discourses around mother-in-law violence against daughters-in-law in India' *Women's Studies International Forum* 34 (5): 420-429. Pergamon.
- Gondolf EW and DM Russel (1987). *Man to Man: A Guide for Men in Abusive Relationships.* New York: Sultzberg and Graham.

- Gupte M (2013). 'Why Feminism Should Inform Our Routine Interventions in Domestic Violence' in *Feminist Counselling and Domestic Violence in India* ed. P Bhate-Deosthali, S Rege, P Prakash. Routledge.
- Hague G & Bridge S (2008). 'Inching forward on domestic violence: The "co-ordinated community response" and putting it in practice in Cheshire'. *Journal of Gender Studies*, 17(3), 185-199.
- Hague G (2013). 'Learning From Each Other: The Special Cell and Domestic Violence Activist Responses in Different Contexts Across the World'. *Violence Against Women* 19(10) 1224–1245. Sage Publications.
- Hamberger LK & Hastings J (1993). 'Courtmandated treatment of men who assault their partner'. In *Legal responses to wife assault: Current trends and evaluation* ed. Hilton Newbury Park, CA: Sage. 188-229.
- Hanmer J (1990). 'Men, power and the exploitation of women' in *Men, masculinities and social theory* ed. J Hearn and D Morgan. London: Unwin Hyman. 21-42.
- Healey KC Smith and C O'Sullivan. (1998) *Batterer intervention: program approaches and criminal justice strategies.* National Institute of Justice. US Department of Justice.
- Heise LL (2011). 'What works to prevent partner violence: An evidence overview'. STRIVE Research Consortium.
- ICRW. (1999) Domestic Violence in India: A Summary Report of Three Studies. Washington: ICRW.
- Jaising I (2009) 'Bringing Rights Home: A Review of the Campaign for a Law on Domestic Violence'. *Economic and Political Weekly* 44 (44).
- Joshi A (2013). 'Healing from Violence: Integrating Feminism and Psychotherapy' in Feminist Counselling and Domestic Violence in India ed. P Bhate-Deosthali, S Rege, P Prakash. Routledge.

- Koenig M A, R Stephenson, S Ahmed, SJ Jejeebhoy, J Campbell (2006). 'Individual and Contextual Determinants of Domestic Violence in North India', *American Journal of Public Health* 96 (1): 132-138.
- Krishnan S (2005). 'Do Structural Inequalities Contribute to Marital Violence? Ethnographic Evidence From Rural South India', *Violence Against Women* 11 (6): 759 – 775.
- Martin D (1976). *Battered Wives.* New York: Pocket Books.
- Ministry of Health and Family Welfare, Government of India. (2006*). National Family Health Survey (NFHS-3) 2005-06.* IIPS and MoHFW. New Delhi: Govt of India.
- Mauricio AM and B Gormley (2001). 'Male perpetrators of physical violence against female partners: The interaction of dominance, needs and attachment insecurity'. *Journal of Interpersonal Violence* (16): 10661081.
- Miller J (2003). 'An Arresting Experiment: Domestic Violence Victim Experiences and Perceptions'. *Journal of Interpersonal Violence.* 18 (7): 695-716.
- Murphy C (2009). *Men's Intimate Partner Abuse and Control: Reconciling Paradoxical Masculinities and Social Contradictions.* Doctoral Thesis, School of Justice, Brisbane.
- Panchal, TJ (2017). *Men, intimate partner violence and change: Feminist social work interventions in the Special Cell.* PhD Thesis submitted in fulfillment of the requirements for the Degree of Doctor of Philosophy in Social Sciences, Tata Institute of Social Sciences, Mumbai.
- Pence E and M Paymar (1993). *Education groups for men who batter: The Duluth Model.* New York, NY: Springer.
- Ranjan P & Dave A (2003). Strategic alliance: A case of the Maharashtra Police, UNIFEM and TISS. Paper presented at the *Fifth Global Meeting of Women and Policing,* Vera Institute of Justice, Brasilia, Brazil.

- Rajan RS (2006). 'Is the Hindu Goddess A Feminist?' in *Feminism In India,* Kali for Women: 318-336.
- Rege, S and Chandrasekhar A (2013). 'Feminist Domestic Violence Interventions in India' in *Feminist Counselling and Domestic Violence in India* ed. P Bhate-Deosthali, S Rege, P Prakash. Routledge.
- Resource Centre for Interventions on Violence Against Women. (Forthcoming). 'Factors Precipitating Women's Help-seeking from the Special Cell: Draft Report'. Tata Institute of Social Sciences.
- Rew M, Gangoli G, & Gill AK (2013). Violence between female in-laws in India. Journal of International Women's Studies, 14(1), 147.
- Sakhrani M & Jhaveri Panchal T (2014). *Quest for justice: A study of the implementation of the Protection of Women from Domestic Violence Act, 2005*. Mumbai, India: Tata Institute of Social Sciences.
- Sen I (1990) 'Introduction' *A Space Within the Struggle*. New Delhi: Kali for Women.
- Solotaroff JL and RP Pande. (2014). *Violence Against Women and Girls: Lessons from South Asia.* South Asia Development Forum, Washington: World Bank.
- Solanki G & Gangoli G (2016). 'Defining Domestic Violence and Women's Autonomy in Law'. *SocioLegal Review* 12 (51).
- Special Cell for Women and Children (2004). *Mission statement and the monitoring indicators for Special Cell for Women and Children: A programme for Curbing violence against women within the state police system*. Mumbai, India: Tata Institute of Social Sciences.
- Special Cell for Women and Children (1994). *Because the personal is political: A documentation of the work of the Special Cell for Women and Children 1984-1994*. Mumbai, India: Tata Institute of Social Sciences.
- Special Cell for Women and Children (forthcoming) *Spirit and Strategies*. Mumbai, India: Tata Institute of Social Sciences.

- Stark E (1996). 'Mandatory Arrest of Batterers: A Reply to Its Critics' in *Do Arrests and Restraining Orders Work?* Ed. Eve S Buzawa and Carl G Buzawa. Sage.
- Thorne-Finch R (1992). *Ending the Silence: The Origins and Treatment of Male Violence Against Women.* Toronto: University of Toronto Press.
- Vindhya U (2013). ' Feminist Counselling for Domestic Violence: Some Issues of Theory and Practice' in *Feminist Counselling and Domestic Violence in India* ed. P Bhate-Deosthali, S Rege, P Prakash. Routledge.
- World Health Organisation. (2017) 'Violence Against Women: Intimate Partner and Sexual Violence Against Women. Factsheet. Available at [http://www.who.int/mediacentre/factsheets/fs239/en/] Accessed on 14 March 2018.

Programme to Commemorate 25 Years of Special Cells

Dr Trupti Panchal addressing the audience, commemorating 25 years of work of Special Cells in Maharashtra.

Prof Meenakshi Apte (Founder of Special Cell) and Dr Armaity Desai (ex-Director, TISS) delivering the inaugural address at the Programme.

Ranjana Gaikwad, Special Cell social worker conducting an awareness session on violence against women with women in Pune (Rural).

Inauguration of Special Cell at Yavatmal district on 2nd July, 2002 by Mr Manikrao Thakarey (then Minister of State, Home Dept, Maharshtra), along with Superintendent of Police, Yavatmal.

Mr Prabhat Ranjan (then Deputy Inspector General of Police-Prevention of Atrocities against Women), at the inauguration of Special Cell for Women and Children, Nasik in 2003.

Special Cell social workers participating with other women's groups in an awareness march and rallies against violence on women in Aurangabad.

The Special Cell Team from 2002 to 2010.

A Series of Police Training Workshops Conducted in 2003-04 titled 'Millennium Vision- Justice Within Reach'.

Series of Police Training for Police personnel at District level titled: New Horiron in Gender Just Policing, organised by Maharshtra State Police & Tata Institute of Social Sciences

Aurangabad Police Training inauguration function

Participants of Training comprising of Public Prosecutors, Police officers, Forensic Experts and Medical Officers of District.

Police Training on Protection of Women from Domestic Violence Act 2005 and CEDAW on 10th March 2006 jointly with Stree Mukti Sangathana (SMS) at Buldhana. In picture Mr Krishna Prakash, Suprintendent of Police, Buldhana and Ms Sharda Sathe of SMS.

YUVAK-YUVATI MELA

Programme on Bending Games for Gender Equality

Young men and women playing games at the mela organised by Special Cell for Women in Aurangabad in 2008.

Women Playing gender Games at the Open House organised by Mumbai Special Cell for former clients in 2007 at Police Club.

Women Playing gender Games at the Open House organised by Special Cell, Wardha for former clients in 2007 at Police Headquaters.

Open House organised by Mumbai Special Cell for former clients.

Yuvati Mela organised by Special Cell Yavatmal for community women in 2007.

Covers of Special Cells publications.